All Things Worked Together for Good

James Ricketts

All Things Worked Together for Good

A real life tale of divine connections

James Ricketts

James Ricketts

Text copyright © December 2019 James Ricketts

The right of James Ricketts has been asserted by him in accordance with the Copyright, Designs and Patents Act 1988.

All rights reserved. No part of this publication may be reproduced or transmitted in any form or by any means, electronic or mechanical, including photocopy, recording, or any information storage and retrieval system, without permission in writing from the publisher.

ISBN 9781703735697

First edition 2019

Acknowledgments

Scripture quotations are primarily taken from the Holy Bible New King James Version®. Copyright © 1982 by Thomas Nelson. Used by permission. All rights reserved.

A catalogue record for this book is available from the British Library

For Janey

James Ricketts

Contents

Introduction	9
Chapter 1 Pushing the Boundaries	11
Chapter 2 The Happiest Days of Your Life?	25
Chapter 3 Would It Ever Happen?	35
Chapter 4 A Narrow Escape	43
Chapter 5 Wedding Bells and a Move South	55
Chapter 6 Hiraeth	67
Chapter 7 Back to School	81
Chapter 8 New Horizons	91
Chapter 9 A New Life Down Under	107
Chapter 10 The Ups and Downs of Life in Paradise	117
Chapter 11 The Reverend James	131
Chapter 12 "I Want What You Want"	145
Chapter 13 Absence Makes the Heart Grow Fonder	157
Chapter 14 Life is a Rollercoaster	167
Postscript	187

James Ricketts

Introduction

"And we know that all things work together for good to those that love God, to those who are the called according to His purpose." (Romans 8:28)

This verse is very special to me. I once spent a while in hospital after a terrible motorcycle accident. When I came to my senses, there were various cards around my bed from well-wishers. One of the first cards I opened was from a friend at my home church, and this verse was written inside it. I realise that the title of this book uses the past tense 'worked', but that's a deliberate strategy as I am looking back at my life retrospectively.

My story clearly illustrates the truth contained in this verse. Sometimes it's hard to see any good in our daily circumstances. However, we don't usually see the whole picture of what's really going on in our lives. We only see a jigsaw piece. Over time, we fit the bits together piece by piece and begin to see the big picture.

This book is a true story about my life. Its purpose is to encourage, amuse, inspire you, and to show how my faith in

God has affected my life and the lives of those around me. Perhaps it will also deter some from making the mistakes I have made.

Let me give you one more verse. This isn't a theological book, but I particularly like this excerpt:

"I am come that they may have life, and that they may have it more abundantly" (John 10:10b).

A lot of people misinterpret this, thinking it means that God intends us to have material wealth. I don't know about that, but I do know there is more than one way to be rich.

Some time ago, while serving as the pastor of a Pentecostal church, I embarked on a sabbatical. Having served for seven years in a bi-vocational capacity, it was time for a break. As I was in full-time secular employment as well as working in the church, I was only able to get away for a few weeks. Having previously lived in New Zealand for some time, I felt drawn to revisit the country and see what God had to say to me there. As it happens, he had quite a lot to say!

One thing I felt challenged to do was write it down. This didn't just apply to a word in season or to God's word at a particular time, but to my whole life experience. When I thought about this, I felt overwhelmed. I realised I had been blessed immeasurably by God and that there had also been many challenges. But where would I start?

I knew that writing everything that had happened in my life would be an enormous task, and I didn't even think it would be that interesting. With that in mind, I only included the life events that have real significance.

Chapter One

Pushing the Boundaries

I was born in Beeston, Nottinghamshire, and had two elder brothers: John and David. My father was serving as the minister of a Pentecostal church in the town; his second pastoral appointment. When I was just four years old he took up a new appointment and we had to move. As a result, I have very little recollection of our life in Beeston, but here are some of the snapshots I can still recall.

I remember family days out at the park and other fun places. My parents never had much money and life was tough in those days. If a visitor came to stay we would put coats or curtains on our beds as the blankets had to go to our visitors. The 'bathroom' was down at the end of the garden. Visitors would be given a torch and told to follow the clothes line if it was dark.

James Ricketts

Dad was paid on Sunday nights and his salary came from the church offering, as that was his full-time job. As a result, there was often little food available by the end of the week. Treats like biscuits, cakes and fizzy drinks were basically non-existent at home, which made life embarrassing for our parents whenever we visited anyone. If a plate of cakes or biscuits came out, whoosh! My brothers and I were all over it like a plague of locusts, and within seconds everything would be gone.

As Dad was on a very meagre wage, he supplemented his wages doing furniture removals and cleaning chimneys. As a result, our family transport was a furniture van, which also served as our holiday home. While we were away we would sleep in the back and cook on a primus paraffin stove.

Our grandma came with us one time and we parked up on a beach in the van. People must have thought it strange to see Grandma sitting on a settee, right there on the beach, doing her knitting. It was odd, a bit eccentric even, but we had a fabulous family life.

I heard a story about a baptism service Dad once held at the church. The baptismal tank was in the floor. It was covered with a wooden lid and the tank was tiled inside. The tiles were dirty and cracked, so Dad decided to put a little drop of green watercolour into the tank to disguise its dishevelled state.

As he went to put the paint in, the whole chunk fell into the water. There was no time to drain and refill it, and it would have needed reheating anyway, so the baptisms went ahead. In those days, people wore white clothing to be baptised. As they rose up from the waters on that occasion there was a distinct tinge of green about them.

All Things Worked Together for Good

In 1969, we moved to Holyhead, an island in North West Wales, as Dad had been appointed minister of a Pentecostal church there. We were given the keys to the manse, a little terraced house not far from the church. Dad had a mini in those days. He was always under the bonnet of his cars, struggling to keep them going. Fortunately, he could fix just about anything.

One morning he noticed the car was gone. It had been stolen. However, one of the few benefits of being a bit poor was that there was never much petrol in the car, so the thief had only managed to get a couple of hundred yards down the lane before it spluttered to a halt!

My brothers and I settled into our new environment quickly. John was the eldest, and he was very clever. He was always inventing or contriving some plan that would get me and David into some sort of trouble. When we started attending school just around the corner, John was nicknamed 'Columbo' by his classmates because he wore a long hand-me-down raincoat from another family member.

David was something of a daredevil. He knew absolutely no fear. Danger was a completely unknown entity to him. Dad would often drive us to the big swimming pool on the mainland, which had a deep end complete with seventeen-foot diving boards. David couldn't even swim at this point, but he would clamber up the steps to the top and jump off. Dad would then have to rescue him and pull him over to the side. He would get straight up there again, and so it went on.

Pain was no deterrent to David either. When he got the slipper or wooden spoon (yes, parents did that in those days, and it taught us respect), David would say "Didn't hurt", which often resulted in another whacking. Dad was a bit of a soft touch, so if there was any discipline to be issued Mum did it, but we were only ever punished when we really deserved it.

Mum sometimes took in lodgers or exchange students. This brought a little extra money in, but it meant that we three boys had to share a bedroom. There was a bunk bed and a single in the room, which Dad had made himself out of timber and webbing. For some reason I liked to go under the single bed and put my legs up through the webbing, pushing the mattress up in the middle. One day when I was doing this, David jumped down onto the single bed from the top bunk. It really hurt and I yelled loudly, as five-year-olds do when they're in pain. It turned out the tibia of my left leg was broken! In later life, David and I would count up who had broken the most bones. He said that I couldn't include the leg bone as I didn't break it. He did!

Every morning on his way down the stairs, David would jump up and grab the bannister rail above him on the landing. He would swing on it before dropping back onto the stairs and walking down. One day he jumped up and missed, flying all the way down the stairs and hitting the floor hard. A panic ensued and an ambulance was called. Thankfully, he escaped with a concussion and a broken wrist. In the long term, he lost some hearing as a result of this escapade.

A year after we arrived in Holyhead my younger brother Simon was born. My birthday was in June and his birthdate was expected to be very close to my sixth birthday. I thought it would be unfair if his birthday was before mine because in my mind, I thought that would somehow place him higher up the scale than me. I hoped he would be late, and he was! He arrived four days after my birthday. At last there was someone younger; someone lower down the pecking order.

As he got a bit older I often picked on him without good reason. As a result, he would scream if I went near him. Then Mum would assume I was hurting him and give me a whacking. Simon soon learned how to use this to his advantage.

One day, we were both at home and Dad needed to pop out in the car. "I have to go out for a while. Don't antagonise him," he warned me as he got in the car.

The car hadn't even made it out of the drive before Simon began screaming. I saw the car stop as soon as Dad heard it. I made myself scarce and ran indoors, locking myself in the bathroom. He forced the door open and grabbed the nearest thing he could – a plastic toy baseball bat – and I was given a few whacks with it. Dad was so gentle, but we often pushed him beyond his limits!

It was only a thin, flimsy bat, but when I got a little older I would tell people, with a sneaky smile, that Dad had beaten me up with a baseball bat, especially when we had special guests. He would throw his hands up in the air and protest: "It was only a plastic one!"

After a few years, Dad decided to step down from church ministry for a while for financial reasons to find secular work. He did this as a last resort, only intending to take a temporarily break from the ministry in order to get on top of our finances.

He soon got a job as the manager of a TV shop and we moved from The Manse to a cottage close to the coast. The cottage was near a hotel and a couple of other houses, but apart from that it was quite isolated.

At the end of the lane near our cottage was a busy main road, and on the other side of this road was a beach with a rocky headland and a number of small coves and cliffs. Mum instructed us that we could go anywhere we liked but that we must never, ever go across the road.

The hotel had a playground and plenty of places to explore in its grounds, so at first the request to stay away from the road and the dangerous cliffs seemed reasonable and we complied with Mum's wishes. Inevitably, though, we were eventually lured in by the mystery of what lay over the road.

We were soon down on the beach exploring the rocks, cliffs and caves, or searching for anything interesting that had been washed up. By this time Dad had a small boat, which was kept on the small beach nearest the cottage. We would sometimes go out in it, rowing out to sea for what seemed like miles. There were no flares, VHF radios or lifejackets; just three boys out having fun.

We had seen some people rock climbing with ropes on television. As Dad was in the TV business, we knew there was some aerial cable in the garage and thought to ourselves, "That'll do." Before long we were climbing down the steepest of cliffs with long drops to the unforgiving jagged rocks below. The more I think about it, the more I realise now that God's hand of protection must have been on us.

We also had a tin bath, back from the times when there had been no bathroom. John decided we should use it as a canoe, so off we went down to the beach. It was a bit unstable and we had to add rocks for ballast. We also weighed ourselves down with rocks sometimes and used a hosepipe to breathe and walk underwater. We even rode our bikes underwater! All the while, our dear parents were blissfully unaware that we had strayed beyond our 'safe' boundaries.

Various random items were washed up onto the beach. One morning we found a large slab of expanded polystyrene. It had probably been part of a life raft from a ship or something. It was very thick, and probably measured about eight feet long and four feet wide. Naturally, we took it home.

To our surprise, Dad decided to take us out on it. We launched it on a big beach just round the coast and tried to paddle it home using bits of driftwood as oars. It was summertime and there were lots of people out on the water in proper boats. Several came alongside us and asked if we were OK. It must have looked like we had been shipwrecked! We kept the raft for many years, although it gradually got smaller and smaller as bits broke off. It was eventually disposed of, but what fun we had with it over the years.

Dad did have a real boat; a fibreglass dinghy with a small outboard. One time we were out in the boat fishing with Uncle Gordon. He always wore a suit and tie, and he looked a bit nervous. I think he had only ever seen fish at the supermarket, so the first time we landed a fish into the boat and it flapped about in the bottom I thought he was going to jump over the side.

As if that wasn't bad enough, Dad was sitting at the back of the boat with his hand on the motor tiller control. His foot was held at an unusual angle out in front of him. Gordon asked, "Derek, why have you got your foot there like that," and he replied, "Oh, there's a hole there." He wasn't joking, either. He moved his foot away and a little fountain of water appeared beneath it.

Further round the coast was an old firing range that had been used to train soldiers during the war. We would walk around and collect the .303 rifle bullets and shell cases that were lying on the pathways and among the gorse bushes. We would then sell these bullets at school. The headmaster eventually found out and put a stop to it, fearing it could be dangerous.

During one visit to the firing range I found what looked like a mortar bomb, complete with fins and everything. In my twelve-year-old mind I thought it would be fun to make it go off. I figured the worst thing that could happen would be me ending up with a black face and my hair on end. In cartoons this was true, but in real life it certainly wasn't, although I was blissfully unaware of this fact. I hurled it as hard as I could at a big rock, waiting for the big bang. I did this again and again. Thankfully, it was a dud and I finally threw it off the cliff and into the sea. I guess I wouldn't be writing this today if it had been a live one.

The hotel would come to life at the start of the holiday season. There was a shop and a games room, and there would be discos in the evenings. Lots of holidaymakers would come and it livened up the whole area. We made good friends with some of the children who visited and would see them year after year.

All Things Worked Together for Good

I once saw a skinhead in the park area sitting on the roundabout. He was eating biscuits. "Give us a biscuit," I said. I didn't know him; I was just trying to be friendly.

He obviously wasn't the friendly type. He got hold of me and started punching and kicking me. I had black eyes, and I was bruised and bleeding. He even got some rope and friction-burned the backs of my legs with it. By the time he had finished with me I was in a right state, and I went home crying my eyes out. Mum was horrified at the sight of me and tended to my injuries.

My brothers and a friend who lived in the hotel vowed to help me get revenge. I didn't always get on with my brothers, but when something like this happened we stuck together. They got hold of the skinhead and held him down while I punched him a few times. I had to stay in the house then until I was sure he had gone home from his holiday!

My brothers and I were regular visitors to the local A&E department. Cuts and scrapes, falls, broken bones; there was always something. I had a habit of smashing bottles and glass behind the garage next to our house. As a result, there was debris and broken glass everywhere.

One year close to bonfire night I bought some bangers with my pocket money. Matches at the ready, I opened the packet and lit the fuse of one and threw it behind the garage. We had two cats at the time, and cats can be inquisitive. One of them went up to the fizzing firework. I was worried the cat might get hurt, so I rushed in to shoo it out of the way.

In my haste to save the wayward feline, I slipped over and landed heavily on a shard of broken glass. I got myself up and out of the way just as the banger went off. I put my hand to my buttock and it was wet, and when I held up my hand it was red. I was bleeding quite heavily from a large gash on my backside, but I was more embarrassed than anything. I eventually realised that I couldn't hide it from my parents any longer and was taken to the hospital to get it seen to. I had to have several stitches.

Another time my cousin Peter was visiting. He lived down south and would often come and stay with us during the summer holidays. He and I were a similar age and got on well, most of the time at least. One day we were messing about in the garden and for some reason he hit me and then ran off. I chased after him and he went through the back door, slamming it quickly behind him. The door consisted of four glass panes. I couldn't stop in time and went crashing through the middle two, landing halfway along the hallway with shattered glass flying everywhere.

Mum came running out. "What have you done? What have you done?" she shouted.

I lay there for a moment. I was OK, but I was bleeding from my left wrist. I was lucky to get away with a couple of bad cuts, and I still have the scars to prove it. I had narrowly missed the main artery, so things could have been a lot worse. We must have been a constant source of worry to our poor parents.

There was a games room in the hotel near our house, so there were lots of one-armed bandits and pinball machines inside. We never had any money, but my brothers and I knew a few little tricks. We would stuff empty crisp packets into the pay-out trays of the one-armed bandits so someone would win but the machine wouldn't pay out. While they went to find someone to complain to, we would come back and remove the wrappers, and the money would come out.

The pool table could be also lifted and dropped in a certain way that sent the balls out without the need for coins. We knew all the tricks and would sometimes go home with our pockets bulging with copper coins.

There was a man called Harry who worked at the hotel and looked after the games room. Although we were a constant nuisance, he was very patient with us. He was a big man and bore a striking resemblance to Demis Roussos, the famous Greek singer. Despite the age difference, we got on well and shared the same taste in music: Pink Floyd, Genesis and bands like that. Sometimes he would sell or lend me his albums.

Harry was into diving and would sometimes go spear fishing. One day he invited me to join him. My brother John had a wetsuit and all the bits and pieces that went with it. He also had a spear gun. I don't remember asking John if I could borrow it, but I made use of it anyway.

We went to the large, sandy beach down the road. The tide was coming in over the hot sand and the water stayed quite warm. The wetsuit was a bit on the big side, but still usable. We snorkelled up and down looking for flatfish. The fish would lie still on the sandy seabed, assuming they were invisible as predators swam over them. The giveaway was their eyes and the trail in the surface sand.

I soon spotted a trail and a pair of eyes. It looked like a big one, so I fired the spear gun at it. It was only an elastic strap and a trigger mechanism with a three-pronged spear, but it was still quite powerful. The spear hit the fish on its head and it shot off away from me, much to my disappointment. It was the one that got away!

But about twenty minutes later I saw the fish lying on its back, stunned, with its white underside showing, making it even easier to hit. I fired the spear into it and pulled it in on the attached line. It was flapping about like mad, so I whacked it over the head with my knife handle and placed it in my string bag, which I had tied to my weight belt.

We had family staying that week. When I brought the fish home Mum was delighted as it weighed nearly four pounds. Potatoes were peeled, chips were made and there was enough plaice and chips for about ten people. Even my brother David, a keen fisherman of the rod and reel type, was really impressed.

Harry and I often went out spear fishing and I rarely came back without a few fish. People who stayed in the hotel on holiday would ask us where the best fishing spots were. We would tell them to fish in a place where we knew they would lose their tackle. Then we would go back there at low tide and collect it.

Another time we were out in the boat fishing. David and John had all the proper fishing gear, while I had an orange crab line with about twenty feet of line on it. I had a spark plug as a weight and a spinner as a lure. The line went tight and I initially thought I had snagged it on a rock. I asked John to stop rowing and he pulled the line in for me. Imagine the look on his face when a large cod came up out of the water! Again, the family was fed from my catch, which I had to admit was a bit of a fluke.

All Things Worked Together for Good

Simon was a bit too young at this point to get involved in our scrapes. He seemed to be constantly running around the garden in his wellies and anorak, hood up, even in summer!

Our next-door neighbours were a lovely older couple. Very patient, they never complained about the constant noise the four of us made or our boisterous behaviour. One day, Simon discovered Granddad's old fireman's axe. He managed to perforate the neighbour's garage door about twenty times before he was found and stopped. Paying for a new door would have been very difficult, but they settled for a repair job, which Dad did himself.

To make ends meet, Mum offered bed and breakfast facilities at our house and the three older boys, myself included, were put into one bedroom to make room for guests. Different people came to stay every week at that time.

Later on, she got a job at the newly built leisure centre. I remember going for a swim at the centre with my friend from next door. I was wearing scruffy clothes and wellington boots, and Mum looked horrified and more than slightly ashamed of me when I arrived. I was told never to come looking like that again!

As a result of Dad being in ministry, we were always at church as youngsters. There were the morning services, Sunday school, evening services, boys' club midweek and various other activities. Sunday school was led by an enthusiastic man called Harold, whose wife was one of the teachers. Week by week we would go along, sing songs, and learn about Jesus and the Bible and the need for salvation. We would sing gospel songs and choruses, and they all had actions. We all sang and did the actions with great enthusiasm and energy.

Every week, Harold would say, "You must accept Jesus Christ as your personal saviour." He emphasised the great importance of this. I had been going to church since I was just a few weeks old but had never made this commitment. It was never something that was forced upon us; we were given the space to make our own minds up.

One Sunday, when I was around eleven years old, I went home to my bedroom alone and prayed the prayer. I asked for forgiveness for my sins and invited Jesus to come into my life, change me and make me more like Him. I never told anyone and didn't really feel any different at the time. I guess nothing much changed in my life during my childhood years, but looking back I can see that God had his hand on my life.

Chapter Two

The Happiest Days of Your Life?

Secondary school seemed like a daunting prospect to me. It was a large comprehensive in the town centre with more than two thousand pupils, and all sorts of stories about the way newcomers were treated had been repeated to me. I was scared. I didn't want to have my head put down the toilet. I didn't want to be forced to take drugs. I didn't want to be beaten up every day or have my dinner money stolen.

As we lived in a remote location, too far away from any bus stops and too far to walk, a taxi was sent out every day to pick us up and take us home again. There were lots of other kids in these outlying areas who also needed picking up. The taxi was an old Morris Oxford, and the driver was a scruffy chain-smoker with green false teeth, who we called 'Honk'.

He probably got this nickname because most mornings we weren't ready, so he would honk his horn impatiently. Sometimes there would be three or four kids in the front seat and as many as ten in the back; none with seatbelts on. One day a door burst open and two little girls fell out. They had been making Mother's Day cards at school and were upset that their cards had been damaged as they rolled down the road. Luckily there were no injuries. It could have been a lot worse!

Honk thought it was funny to squeeze the top of my legs hard, to the point that it caused me pain. Sometimes he would take his horrible green false teeth out and wave them in our faces. On one occasion he twisted my arm up behind my back. It really hurt and he wouldn't stop, so I punched him in the face with my other hand and sent his glasses flying. He hurled abuse and threatened to report me as I ran off.

Later that day, I realised he actually had reported me and I was summoned to the headmaster's office. When such a thing happened the errant pupil would be forced to wait outside the office silently, facing the wall and contemplating his or her sorry fate. Eventually, the door swung open and I was faced with the huge frame of Mr Llewellyn Jones; a man feared by even the cockiest troublemakers.

He instantly began bellowing at me. I tried to explain the injustices of having cigarette smoke blown over me, the leg squeezing, the taking out of the green teeth (and the waving of them in our faces) and the arm twisting, but it was to no avail. A tirade of yelling ensued.

All Things Worked Together for Good

During the yelling, I noticed a filing cabinet to my left. It had a series of dents in the side. Over to my right was another in a similarly dented condition. I wondered, 'How this could be?' and I soon found out. I was picked up by my lapels and hurled across the office into one of the filing cabinets, then picked up again and thrown into the other one. Finally, I was picked up and given a good hiding in the traditional fashion. I never mentioned this to my parents as I figured I had probably asked for it.

I was never a model pupil, but I was considered bright enough to be in the upper stream. However, I was easily distracted and had a short attention span. I guess I would have been labelled with ADHD or similar if I was at school today. Thankfully, there were opportunities to get involved in other things that were of interest, like music.

I come from quite a musical family. Dad played the piano, ukulele, and even the spoons on his knee. John played the piano and flute, and David played the trumpet.

In music class, we were all asked, "Who would like to learn a musical instrument?"

I put my hand up.

"What would you like to play?" the music teacher asked.

"Saxophone," I replied.

"Here, have a trumpet," he said, handing me a battered case.

And that was that. There was no discussion; I would learn the trumpet.

We were expected to take the instrument home to practise. Once a week, a specialist music teacher would come to teach the chosen instrument on a one-to-one basis.

James Ricketts

This involved missing a half-hour lesson in another subject and copying up the notes afterwards.

My parents were very supportive of my new hobby and I seemed to be progressing well. I had also been signed up for piano lessons, but never really enjoyed them. After three years learning piano I still couldn't play many tunes. It wasn't really for me and I was finally allowed to stop, but I continued with my trumpet playing. I eventually worked my way up to playing first trumpet in the school band and also played in the local Youth Orchestra.

Everyone in my class was given a sponsorship form. It seemed the school needed extra funds for something and we were all down to do a twenty-length sponsored swim. Mum had been working as a lifeguard at the leisure centre for a while and we all knew how to swim, so I started taking the form round our church members and people gladly signed up as sponsors.

I did the twenty lengths easily, then collected in the monies and popped the pile of coins on my bedroom shelf. No one ever asked me for the money; it just sat there. I never intended to be dishonest, but as no one had asked for the money my twelve-year-old mind figured it was mine. Simple as that.

Skateboarding was popular in the 70s, but boards were expensive. A reasonable one cost about twelve pounds, which, coincidentally, was about the amount I had raised from the swim. I took myself off to the sports shop in town one lunchtime to buy a board.

Sadly, I was a bit short. But seeing my collection of coins and the disappointment on my face the shopkeeper assumed the money I had was the result of many months of scrimping and saving, and he let me have the board at a reduced price. Likewise, my parents were very proud of me for saving up all my pocket money. I didn't tell them the truth for many years! I have since made a donation to a charity associated with the school, in order to recompense, allowing for 40 years of inflation!

My brothers and I, along with some of the other local kids, were always out and about exploring. We were messing about among the bushes on some waste ground one day when something caught my eye in the undergrowth. It was grey and oval and had strange holes in it. I initially thought it was a beehive or something. I put a stick inside it and plucked it out of the ground to get a better look. To our surprise, it was a skull. A human skull! We were dancing around with it still on the end of the stick, pretending we were head-hunters from a faraway tribe. John wanted to make a desk lamp out of it, but I reminded him that it was mine.

We arrived home thinking it quite normal to have a skull on a stick, but our parents were horrified, and the police were called. The skull was removed, dashing John's hopes of turning it into a desk lamp. The skull had to be taken away by the police and tested. We later learned that it was three hundred years old and female.

Sometime later there was a big storm. After a large storm like this, interesting objects would often be washed up. On this occasion, we decided to go to the big sandy beach down the road. We were surprised to find a number of human bones and skulls on the sand over at the far end of the beach. Again, the police were called. The bones were picked up, put into bags and taken away. It turned out the storm had washed away the graves from an ancient burial ground up on the headland on this occasion. A special fenced-off area was constructed, and the bones were reinterred with a memorial at the site.

I was offered the chance to go to an outdoor activity centre with the school. This involved staying at a place on the other side of Anglesey, near the Menai Straits. I was told there would be canoeing, swimming, mountaineering and all sorts of other activities. Most of the class signed up.

On arrival we were sent to our dormitories: one for the girls and one for the boys. Each day we would go out somewhere in the back of a Land Rover. It was an exciting time.

On one occasion, we were taken to a nearby beach.

"Right then, who's sailed a boat before?" asked the instructor.

I put my hand up, as did one or two others.

"Off you go, then," he said, pointing towards several single-sailed dinghies sitting on launch trailers.

When I said I had sailed a boat, this wasn't exactly true. I had sailed *in* a boat before, but not on my own. I knew the basics and Dad had taken us out sailing several times in his big catamaran, but I had never actually sailed by myself.

I pushed the craft off from the shore. I knew that as soon as the waters were deep enough I would need to push the daggerboard and rudder down. I did this and set the main sail, holding the mainsheet in my hand and the tiller in the other. The wind soon filled the sail and I moved off. Suddenly it was going so fast I had to lean out to counterbalance it, just like a pro! I turned and tacked into the wind. There was nothing to it.

As I grew in confidence, I moved further and further up the straits. When it was the time to go back in and prepare for our evening meal, I turned around and headed for shore. The wind was behind me and I appeared to be moving quite quickly. The problem was, the tide had turned and the flow against me was stronger than the wind behind me. No matter how hard I tried, I was dragged further and further out to sea.

By this point I was worried. I was only about eleven or twelve, and I felt my life was in real danger. I was crying and panicking about what would happen to me. Eventually, the inshore lifeboat came out and towed me back to safety. My classmates could see that I was shaken. They were kind to me, put my boat away and gave me a warm coat. What a relief it was to be back on dry land. I realised I needed to learn to think before opening my mouth!

My maths class was taken by a notoriously no-nonsense teacher, Mr Roy. I liked him. If two people were talking he would pull their ties together so their faces were about an inch apart, then tie a huge knot in them. Sometimes he would throw the chalkboard duster at pupils' heads or pat their heads with the duster so their hair was covered in white chalk dust.

I was caught misbehaving on one occasion. I can't recall what it was, but I had clearly annoyed Mr Roy.

"Ricketts! Out here!" he bellowed.

James Ricketts

I nervously obeyed, looking sorry for myself. He led me by the tie to a stationery cupboard, which he opened. I was ordered to stand on tiptoes and rest my chin on the top shelf. Bang! The two cupboard doors were slammed against the back of my head, trapping me in there. Then he proceeded to whack me on the backside with a piece of rope. This was most entertaining for the rest of the class and I soon learned that you didn't mess with Mr Roy. I always regarded him as a very good teacher, even though he was a bit unconventional.

On another occasion, I was in geography class. The teacher, Mr Bagnall, was wearing a pair of tan-coloured cowboy boots. I thought they looked ridiculous and pointed them out to the rest of the class. Everyone was laughing except Mr Bagnall. He moved in my direction and I darted off round the desks. He would come one way, trying to get hold of me, and I would go the other. He had no chance.

Finally, with an air of authority, he said: "Right, Ricketts. Over here!"

He was serious at this point so I thought I had better comply. He had a metre rule in his hand – one of those square-section plastic ones – ready to whack me. I was told to hold out my hand, and I obeyed.

He brought the stick down hard, but at the last millisecond I moved my hand out of the way and the stick hit the desk, shattering into a thousand pieces. He had really lost control of the situation and the whole class was laughing. I was ordered out of the classroom, so I went for a nice walk around the school instead of sitting in my lesson.

All Things Worked Together for Good

I used to think a teacher's life was easy with all those long weeks off over the summer and only working from nine to three thirty. In hindsight, I would say teachers need the long break to recover their sanity after having to put up with unruly pupils like me! How much harder the job must be without the threat of a good whacking as a deterrent.

My eldest brother, John, had successfully completed a craft apprenticeship at a nearby factory and was awarded a scholarship to continue his studies and become an engineer. David was halfway through an apprenticeship as a toolmaker at another factory.

I really wasn't sure what I wanted to do, but I seemed to be quite good with my hands. I excelled at things like metalwork, woodwork and technical drawing. I was also quite good at science. Maths was a weak subject for me, as was physics.

The physics teacher, Mr Roberts, seemed to have taken a dislike to me. I never quite understood what he was trying to explain, and my homework always ended up on the 'bad' pile.

One day I was sitting in class on the receiving end of a verbal tirade, and my friend Stuart was sitting there with a smug grin on his face as his book was on the good pile. He didn't escape the wrath, however.

"You!" the teacher yelled at him. "What are you smiling about? Your ears should be sticking out at ninety degrees, picking up as much information as possible!"

I ended up getting an E at 'O' level, while Stuart got a D. Unfortunately for him, He retook his exam in the autumn and got an E like me!

James Ricketts

I handed my trumpet back to the music department on the last day of school and thought nothing more of it. Stuart and I spent the afternoon in my back garden burning our school books in the incinerator in celebration of our newfound freedom.

Despite my academic shortfalls, I achieved good grades in science and technical subjects, and to my surprise I was offered an apprenticeship at the aluminium smelter my brother John had just left.

That meant I had the entire summer to relax and enjoy, knowing I had a good job starting at the end of the break. As I had just turned sixteen I applied for my provisional driving licence. I remember looking at it when it arrived. The expiry date was 2034. It seemed like an eternity away!

Dad offered to lend me the money to buy my first motorbike. At sixteen, the only option was a 50cc model. In those days, the new vehicle registration came out on August 1 every year, so I chose a brand new red Suzuki and picked it up on August 1, 1980.

I rode and rode that bike, taking only a week to rack up the required five hundred miles to 'run in' the engine. Sadly, it mysteriously disappeared from outside the church one Sunday night just before Christmas that year. I was most upset. At the police station they thought it was funny that it had been stolen from outside the church and made jokes about it. Dad and I scoured the town, but it was gone.

Chapter Three

Would It Ever Happen?

I started work as an apprentice the following September and the first year involved full-time study at a technical college. Eight of us started at the same time. Some would be mechanics, others fitters and the rest electricians. I had expressed an interest in becoming a mechanical fitter like John. A couple of weeks into the job, it was decided that I was to be an electrician. I was horrified.

"But I failed physics!" I protested to the instructor.

He just shrugged his shoulders and assured me that it didn't matter.

By this point I was an active member of the church youth group. I would come to college in a denim jacket with sewn-on badges saying things like 'One Way – Jesus' along with a pocketful of tracts. I would stick leaflets in people's coat pockets and in their lunchboxes, and generally annoyed everyone around me.

I was punched, sworn at and shunned by most of the people in my group. I thought it was persecution because of my faith and strong Christian witness. I know now that it was simply because I was an immature Christian going about things the wrong way.

On one occasion I was hung on a coat hook by my overalls and nearly choked. Another time I was locked in a chest freezer. It wasn't persecution; it was because I was annoying. However, this difficult experience caused me to be less open about my faith, and instead I became more like my peers.

John was studying for his engineering degree in Liverpool and became involved in the youth group at a church there. As a result, they would all come down to North Wales on occasion and we would go on a retreat together: all the youth from our church and all the youth from the Liverpool church.

The first time we went away I was encouraged to bring my bass guitar, which I had been learning to play. I didn't think I was good enough, but I was encouraged to join the music team and have a go. They would sing and play for hours, and I began to enjoy playing. Sometimes people would pray, read the Bible or say a few words between songs. Occasionally someone would give a word of prophecy or a word of knowledge, or they would share a vision they had seen.

All Things Worked Together for Good

During one evening meeting I had a distinct sense that someone there had an eye problem. I was nervous about speaking out, but I mentioned it to one of the leaders, who quietened everyone down and explained that I had something to say. With no way out, I nervously explained what I was feeling, and a girl came out to the front straight away. I was told to pray for her, which I did. I don't know whether she was healed or not, but I know God was speaking that day.

At the end of the first year at technical college we underwent a week's intensive first aid course. Considering that we were entering the world of heavy industry, it was deemed necessary to have a good grasp of first aid and CPR, mainly because of the inherent dangers likely to be encountered in such a line of work.

By this time I had a bigger bike, as did my friend Stuart. We spent a lot of time riding around together. I had been bragging to him about the first aid course I had done. I was practically a paramedic in my own eyes! One night we were riding round some narrow country roads and Stuart's front wheel caught the grassy area at the side of the lane. He came off his bike, sliding along the grass. Then he just lay there, motionless.

I panicked. I dropped my bike, ran over and, with no thought for the previous week's training, I grabbed him by his leather jacket and started shaking him violently, yelling, "Stuart, Stuart! Are you all right?"

Thankfully, he was OK. In fact, he just lay there knowing he was unhurt to see what I would do! I saw the funny side of it, so we just straightened out his bike and rode home. It was a good job he wasn't injured, as all the shaking I did could have made things a lot worse for sure.

That summer, I started working at the factory learning my trade on the tools. It was much better than college. The days of bad treatment at the hands of my peers were well behind me and things were totally different.

I had booked a week at the annual Bible Week camp with the other youth from my church. This consisted of us travelling down to Surrey, where the hosting church's Bible College was located. The church had a minibus and it was loaded up with camping gear before we headed off on the three-hundred-and-fifty-mile trip. Meetings were held in a large marquee every day, with specially invited speakers and music groups.

Despite being seventeen, having a good job and owning a motorcycle, one thing was missing. There was no girlfriend on the scene. I just didn't seem to be able to attract anyone. Although Stuart attended my church he didn't come on the trip. But he said something strange to me before we set off: "You'll meet someone there. You'll see." I thought nothing of it as we set off.

We arrived and set up camp. The previous year some of our youth had gone to the same camp and made friends with another group from the South West. For some reason they referred to this group as the 'Rock on Tommies'. I guess they liked comedy duo Cannon and Ball. This group had also arrived and were putting up their tents on the other side of the field. They thought dragging an old fridge with a fire lit inside it over to our camp in the middle of the night to smoke us out of our tents was hilarious.

All Things Worked Together for Good

They would also drive their cars around the field and annoy the other campers, then drive over to our tents at night with their headlights on. After that they would turn the lights off and drive to their own camp. This gave other guests the impression that we were the ones causing the disturbance, and we started receiving complaints.

Their group consisted of several members of a large family, along with some of their friends. There was a brother and several sisters among them, and the girls were all very pretty. For some reason they were always singing: *'Hey Mister Tallyman, tally me banana, Daylight come and me wan' go home'* in perfect tune, and with all the harmonies.

One of the sisters was of a similar age to me and really nice-looking, with blonde hair. I found out that her name was Janey. We spent some time together chatting. I remember that on the day of Charles and Diana's wedding she sat with me to watch it on TV in the cafeteria. She even bought me a cup of tea, but again I thought nothing of it. In those days I had a pretty low self-image and little in the way of self-esteem. I did not expect people to like me. I don't know where that way of thinking came from, but it stayed with me for a long time.

Our paths crossed a good few times that week. On the last day when we were getting the minibus loaded up to drive back down to our camp after the meeting she got into our minibus and sat with me. I didn't get the hint. Then we ended up walking up and down the field under the pretext of looking for someone, and I still didn't get the hint.

Eventually, she slipped an arm around me and said something like, "Looks like I'll have to make the first move!"

James Ricketts

I couldn't believe it. How could someone so beautiful be interested in someone like me?

We spent most of the evening together, sitting and talking around the campsite until the early hours. We savoured our last few hours together. Janey and I exchanged phone numbers and addresses, realising we lived more than three hundred miles away from each other. How would that work out? How often would we see each other? I didn't know how it would work out, but I knew that all my prayers had been answered. Somehow, Stuart's parting words to me as I left for the camp had come true.

We said our goodbyes and went our separate ways. On one hand I was saddened by the knowledge that I wouldn't see her again for a long time, but on the other I was floating on air. I was teased about it all the way home by the others.

On my return, all I got from Stuart was: "I told you, I told you."

All I could think about was when I would see her again. I contemplated a trip on my motorcycle. However, it would have been a long trip to make on my small machine, and with no full licence it would mean I couldn't use any motorways.

We exchanged letters several times a week and phone calls when we could. After a few weeks it was decided that she would come and visit me for a week or so, travelling up by bus. The weeks passed very slowly. After what seemed like an eternity, she arrived one Friday night and I took her home to meet the family.

We stayed out late that night. There were some bus shelters along the seafront with nice ornate roofs on them, so we sat in there enjoying each other's company until the early hours.

Suddenly, a car screeched to a halt next to us. A well-known local gangster got out with about six others. They started hassling us and asking questions.

"Who's the talent?" asked the ringleader.

Janey answered with her name.

"You're going out with *him*?" he questioned, pointing at me and looking surprised.

They picked me up and started laying into me, then threw me over a wall. I got up and we both ran.

They jumped back in the car and gave chase, so we hid in a garden behind some shrubs. The car drove up and down the street looking for us. Eventually, we made it back to the house safely. It wasn't the best way to make a first impression! I shudder to think what they would have done if they had caught us.

Thankfully, the rest of our time together was more pleasant. As I could only take so many days off work I wasn't around much during the day. Janey would walk into the town or stay at the house and play the piano. As the day of her departure drew closer, all we could think about was when we would see each other next.

Mum was concerned that we seemed to be getting 'serious', even though I was still very young. At seventeen I didn't feel young. I had a career, I had a motorcycle, and I had a lady friend. I wasn't some kid any more.

The next few months saw us jumping on trains or blagging lifts; anything to be together. We managed to see each other about once a month. Janey's home was an old farmhouse in the country. It was in a small village, and quite remote. As I entered the house for the first time I found a large open kitchen diner with people everywhere. This was a very large family indeed!

Chapter Four

A Narrow Escape

I passed my motorcycle test the next year, so I finally had a full licence. I bought a bigger bike, and in the February Janey came to visit. It was great having transport and being able to ride around on the bike together, going wherever we wanted without having to rely on anyone else for transport. When the week was over I took her to the station to get a train home. I planned to visit her on the bike that Easter.

James Ricketts

Meanwhile, David had got engaged to Sharon, whom he had known since the first day our family arrived in Holyhead back in 1969. The wedding took place during the first week of April and then I had about ten days off work to go to Devon on the bike.

I fitted a luggage rack to the bike and strapped a rucksack onto it, then set off for the three-hundred-and-thirty-mile ride to Devon. The trip involved riding on a motorway, which was something I hadn't done before. As it was still cold I made a few stops along the way to thaw out. I don't remember much about my time in Devon, but as it happens it turned out to be a longer stay than planned.

On my last night there we rode out to Janey's sister's house and had a meal there. I remember having curry and it being a most enjoyable dinner. Later that evening I decided to go down to the village about two miles away to make a phone call. Being the early eighties, we didn't have the luxury of mobile phones. I wanted to call in on my cousin Peter on the way home the next day, so I headed off to the phone box to make the arrangements while Janey stayed at the house.

As I left, I said something like, "See you in a minute."

She told me later that she sensed something was wrong right from that moment and immediately felt on edge.

It seemed to Janey that I was taking too long to come back from making the phone call. I know I made the call, because Peter later told me I had. She heard the sound of sirens, and blue flashing lights could be seen at the house where we had enjoyed the curry. A house had caught fire in the next village, and the flames could be seen through the window of the house where Janey was anxiously waiting.

All Things Worked Together for Good

In those days it was possible to eavesdrop on the emergency services via FM radio. It was concluded that my lateness in returning was due to my inquisitive nature and that I had probably gone to take a look at the house fire.

The truth would soon become apparent. As soon as they tuned into the police waveband, my name was clearly heard being read out from my driving licence by a police officer. There had been some kind of accident down the road.

Janey said to her sister, "My God! My James!"

She ran outside and flagged down a passing car, which took them to the scene of the crash about half a mile from the house. By this point an ambulance was on the scene and I was being attended to.

I have no recollection of the accident whatsoever. All the information I have is what I was later told by people who had witnessed the aftermath. It seems that I was coming back from making the phone call, travelling on a long, straight section. I must have opened the bike up but failed to take the corner, possibly sliding on gravel as I tried to turn.

As a result, I was launched from the grass verge like a take-off ramp and travelled some one hundred and thirty-five feet, coming to rest on a fallen tree in the field. The bike crashed through the trees and bushes before ending up wrapped around the gatepost. Had the bike landed elsewhere, in the field, for example, it's likely that no one would have seen it and I would not have been found in time.

Just up the road was a garage, but as it was ten p.m. it was closed. A young man and his friend who were walking past the scene and saw the wrecked bike ran to the garage to alert the owner, who lived on the premises. He acted straight away and dialled 999. If he had gone to look before making the call it's likely that the ambulance would have arrived too late.

The police officers tasked with investigating the incident estimated my speed to have been over 80mph. When I hit the tree, the stump of a broken-off branch entered my side. The jagged wood ripped into my flesh and smashed into the ribs on my left side, lacerating my intestines and colon, and tearing the blood vessels and arteries. Blood was pumping into my abdominal cavity from all the damage.

I had also broken my collar bone, dislocated my left shoulder and suffered a head injury. My left arm was hanging behind me due to the dislocation, and the sleeve of my leather jacket had been torn off by the force of the impact. Despite this, I had managed to get off the tree I was partially impaled on and was reportedly crawling around the field, pathetically calling out for Janey, as in all the confusion I clearly thought she had been on the bike and was somewhere nearby.

Because of the house fire in the next village, an ambulance was already on standby and wasn't required there as no one had been injured. A quick radio message diverted the ambulance to the scene of my accident. I was later told that if the ambulance had come all the way from town ten miles away I would have bled to death in that field.

I was rushed to the North Devon District Hospital, where I was taken straight to the emergency room to try to stabilise my condition and get some blood into me. They also needed to reset my dislocated shoulder. I was heard shouting "F*** off!" to the medical professionals as they tried to hold me down. Then, in the next moment, I was pathetically crying out, "Help me, God!"

The operating theatre had just been cleaned after an operation and the surgeon was about to go home at the end of his shift. I was rushed into theatre for urgent surgery.

By this time, word had got back to Janey's mum, who had the task of ringing my parents to tell them what had happened. Trying to soften the blow a bit, she said that I'd had "a bit of a bump". It was late in the evening and Dad was due to start his nightshift. He was just getting up when the phone rang, so he was ready for an overnight drive to Devon.

When they arrived at the hospital in the morning I was just coming out from a six-and-a-half-hour operation. My intestines and colon were so badly damaged that the surgeon had been forced to remove several feet of my insides. Other bits and pieces were taken out and some serious patching up was needed.

I was then placed in the intensive care unit. I was in such a state that I couldn't breathe without a ventilator. I was also receiving regular blood transfusions. I was given eleven pints of blood in total. In addition, I was facing kidney failure, a head injury and the real possibility of brain damage.

Things were not looking good and the odds of survival were stated as "less than fifty-fifty". There was very little chance of me resuming a normal life after this ordeal. My life was literally hanging in the balance.

Mum wanted answers. In her typical fashion, she went to see the surgeon and demanded to know what was going on. The surgeon was in the middle of an operation and a nurse said he was too busy to speak to her. She waited anyway and the surgeon came out still scrubbed up holding his hands up in the air. The first thing he said was "for a start, he should be dead". Then he explained that he didn't know for sure if my intestines were back in the correct place as they had been battling through the night to save my life. He expected that more surgery would be needed as it was very likely that there would be complications.

A few days later, my boss from the aluminium smelter rang the hospital to ask about my condition and to find out when he could expect to see me back at work.

"Don't expect him back this year," he was told. It was only April.

I was expected to be in the hospital for several months, followed by a stay at a hospital closer to home once I was well enough to make the trip. However, word had got out about the accident by this point. As a result, people from churches all over the country were now praying for a miracle.

After the operation I remained in a coma for about a week. I don't remember much about being in the intensive care other than waking up and seeing oscillating fans at the head of my bed. I'm told that I kept saying, "Oh boy!" for some reason.

Soon after this I regained consciousness. A police officer visited me and asked me to sign a statement. The implication was that I must have been under the influence of drink or drugs at the time of the accident. To the police this seemed to be the only explanation for the crash. Thankfully, Dad was there, and as I was still a minor he made sure I signed nothing. I later received a letter from the police saying no further action would be taken as I had been punished enough through my injuries.

Apart from the internal injuries, there were concerns about pressure on my brain as there was some swelling. The surgeons discussed more surgery which would have involved drilling a hole in my skull to relieve the pressure. They didn't think I was well enough to make the ninety mile trip to South Devon where the hospital there had a CT scanner. However, after a few days the decision was made for me to be taken by ambulance to the other hospital in South Devon for the scan.

Mum and Dad followed the ambulance in the car. Thankfully, there was no permanent damage, but there was some bruising to the brain tissue. A few days later I was transferred from intensive care to a surgical ward, and it was there that I began to regain my senses and realise the seriousness of situation I was in. A few days later I was able to get out of bed and walk around. The doctors were amazed.

There were many cards around my bed and I began reading them. The first one I opened contained a verse from the New Testament. It read:

"And we know that all things work together for good to those that love God, to those who are the called according to his purpose." (Romans 8:28)

I wondered at the time how this could possibly apply to me. In later life, with the huge benefit of hindsight and life experience, it made perfect sense.

I came to realise that whatever the situation, and however bad the mistakes we make, God is able to take it and make something good out of it. I know the accident was probably my own fault, although I will probably never know all the details. But God is always there to pick up the pieces when we fail. Even though we may have messed up through our own stupidity or bad judgement, something good can come out of it and we are then able to give God the glory for it.

I was recovering well, but my mind was kind of fuzzy and I had amnesia. A trolley would come around every morning with snacks and newspapers on it. There was a notice on my bed that said: 'Nil by mouth'. I was on a drip and was absolutely starving, so I asked for some Cadbury's Fruit & Nut and a bag of sweets. I managed to eat most of the chocolate before someone stopped me. Oops! The doctors didn't even know if my intestines would work, and there I was eating chocolate with nuts in it. I remember being in terrible pain for a while, but thankfully I survived the ordeal.

People visited me most days and there was talk of an engagement. I didn't remember proposing to Janey, but it allegedly happened the day before the accident. We both knew it was meant to be – God-ordained, even – so who was I to say I knew nothing about it?

My digestive system finally started working again. The blood infection from the internal damage cleared up, my kidneys began to function and I started to make an amazing recovery. An Iranian surgeon who had done a lot of the work on me shook his head in disbelief and said, "All this time is extra" in broken English. What he meant was, I shouldn't have been there. I shouldn't even have been alive.

In less than three weeks I was well enough to be discharged, probably partly due to my badgering the doctors every day, asking when I could get out. Dad made the trip

All Things Worked Together for Good

down again and we stayed the night at Janey's. Then he brought me back to the hospital the next day. I returned to the intensive care unit to thank the staff there for looking after me so well. The look on their faces when I walked in was amazing. They couldn't believe I was back on my feet, alive and well. I showed my gratitude with a card and some chocolates.

Next, I was taken back to the scene of the accident. I stood at the side of the road looking at the scene in disbelief. A diagonal swathe had been cut through the bushes and trees where the bike had left the road. I stood there and experienced a deep sense of eternity and destiny. My life could quite easily have ended there that night. How would I have stood before God? I knew right there and then that I needed to totally recommit my life to Christ.

Dad drove me home in his battered Austin 1800, and Janey also came back with us. She sat in the front, while I lay on the back seat. I was continually tired. My body needed lots of rest as it healed up. All I knew was that the exhaust was blowing and making a terrible noise all the way home. Poor Dad. He had tried to do a makeshift repair, but it was no good. I felt guilty about all the worry and expense I had put him through.

A few weeks earlier there had been a problem getting my wrecked bike back home. Mum and Dad had stayed in a room at the hospital until I was in a stable condition and then planned to travel home for a while. An amazingly practical man, Dad always came up with novel ideas when faced with a problem.

He had taken the front passenger seat out of the car, removed the bike's fuel tank and front wheel, and put them in the boot, along with the front seat. He had then somehow fitted the motorcycle inside the car with the back wheel on the rear seat and the headlight resting against the dashboard on the passenger side. I only saw the photographs, but it looked incredible. Poor mum had been forced to sit in the back behind Dad.

Everyone was really pleased to see me when I got home. I showed off my scars and all the bandages around my abdomen. I had a banging headache, and my shoulder and ribs were still very sore. The church pastor came over to see me, as did some other friends, but all I wanted to do was sleep. I was so tired. Because of the amnesia I kept forgetting what I had said, and ten minutes later I would say the same thing again. This must have been very annoying for everyone else!

The next day I needed to get a lot of prescription items. Dad took me to the town centre chemist in the car and people were really surprised to see me. Holyhead is a small town, and news travels fast. Some had even thought I was dead. It felt strange. A district nurse was soon assigned to me. She came to the house every day to check on me and change my dressings.

Because of the amnesia I couldn't remember much of the college work I had been doing for my apprenticeship and had to repeat a whole year of study! But I gradually got better and stronger.

One afternoon I decided to try to fix my bike. Unfortunately, I hadn't been able to afford fully comprehensive insurance due to my age, so I had to repair it myself. The frame was bent, the tank was dented right in where it had been crushed by the gatepost, and lots of bits and pieces were smashed. There was even some turf still sticking out from under the engine!

I got hold of a blowlamp and a scaffolding pipe to heat up the bent frame. I managed to bend it roughly back into place. The rear light and the part that held the number plate were missing, so I rigged up an old rear fog light to the brake light and taped the number plate to the back of the seat. The bike was just about legal and roadworthy!

I put my gear on, grabbed my helmet and sat on the bike. Then I pressed the starter and the engine burst into life.

Mum came rushing out looking horrified and cried, "What are you doing?"

Most people assumed I would never want to ride a bike again after such a horrific crash. The thing is, I remembered nothing about the crash, so I had no fear of getting back on it.

"I'm going for a ride on my bike," I replied calmly.

I put it into gear and roared away. It was just three weeks after I had come home from hospital. I remember riding up a long, straight road nearby and being surprised that the bike would only do 80mph. It had been such a long time since I had ridden it that I had forgotten it had six gears, not five. I clicked it up into sixth and was soon doing a full ton, still bandaged up! I had no fear of riding and it felt great to be back on the bike, even though it looked a mess.

After just three months my doctor said that I was well enough to go back to work. This was good news, as I was starting to get bored. The only ill-effect I was experiencing at this time was a temporary blackout when I got up too quickly. This was due to anaemia; a hangover from the blood transfusion.

I felt that it was important to give some blood back as soon as I could. I went to the town hall, where they were taking blood from people. Unfortunately, I was told that I would have to wait at least two years before being able to donate any.

Chapter Five

Wedding Bells and a Move South

I visited Janey in Devon a couple more times by train that year. It soon became apparent that we wanted to be together all the time. One solution was for her to move to Holyhead, so later that year I found her a flat. A good friend of mine drove me down to Devon in his mum's car to pick her up with all her belongings.

Just before Christmas, we officially got engaged. We had a party and people seemed to be happy for us. Because of what had happened earlier that year, I guess I had a sense that life was short, and that there was no point hanging around waiting. We initially planned to get married after a couple of years; perhaps once I had completed my apprenticeship and had a good, steady job. Our friends advised us that long engagements were a good idea, but I wasn't so sure.

We started saving for the wedding and married life. I had never really saved before, so I was used to spending every penny I earned. Now things were different. I had a goal. The money soon mounted up.

I even sold my bike for the cause! This turned out to be a rash move as I needed transport and ended up buying another, but before long we had enough money for a house deposit. We found a small house that suited our needs and, at the age of just eighteen, we bought it. My parents had assumed that the wedding would be a long way off, but once we had bought the house I announced that we would be getting married that August.

I expected a lecture; disapproval even. Mum just smiled and said something about summer weddings and buying a new outfit. Dad was always practical and said something like, "You just wait till all the bills come rolling in!" He didn't want to put me off, but neither did he want me to be unprepared for the financial challenges that lay ahead. It turned out they had already put two and two together and concluded that the buying of a house meant we would be marrying sooner rather than later.

My grandmother had been living at my parents' house. She was terminally ill with cancer and had been taken into hospital by this point. I realised she probably wouldn't be alive by the time we were married. This was a stressful time for Mum, as it seemed likely that there would be a wedding and a funeral quite close together. My grandmother passed away a couple of months before we were due to marry.

All Things Worked Together for Good

We had decided to get married in Devon. As Janey's parents had been in the Salvation Army, we arranged to have the wedding at the local corps. She liked the idea of having a wedding photograph taken under the Salvation Army flag.

Money was tight, but our families rallied around us. The wedding dress was handmade by one of Janey's sisters, and Janey's mum made the cake. The reception was a simple buffet in the hall adjoining the Salvation Army church. I think the whole wedding cost something like £200.

It was very hot on the day, and the ceremony was at noon. I was taken to the church in Dad's car. I nervously waited at the front with my best man, Stuart. Noon came and went, and Janey was nowhere to be seen. Finally, after a forty-minute wait, the music started and everyone stood to their feet. I turned to see her walking in slowly on the arm of her brother. She looked absolutely stunning.

After the wedding and reception, we all went to the beach. It was a bit unusual, but we have always liked to be different. I enjoyed taking a swim and having the chance to chat with our guests. Janey's brother finally dropped us off at the hotel. We couldn't really afford a proper honeymoon on an apprentice wage, so we were only booked in for one night. As there were lots of practical jokers in the family, I booked it under a false name. The next day when we checked out I handed the receptionist my bank card to pay the bill. She looked at me and then at the name on the card. She gave me a funny look, but I didn't offer an explanation.

A while later I was asked to go on a course for work. This involved me and two colleagues travelling up north for a week. Janey travelled to Devon while I was away, and I promised to join her for a few days on my return so we could travel back to Holyhead together. My colleagues and I stayed in a hotel and had a hire car to get about.

We had made arrangements that I would phone Janey at a certain time on the Wednesday evening. I didn't want to use the phone in the hotel lobby as I was sure my colleagues, who thought it amusing that I had married so young, would be listening in. To get a bit of privacy I walked fifty yards up the road to a phone box. I rang Janey's mum's number only to be told she had gone out somewhere with her sister.

I thought it was a bit strange, as we normally stuck with arrangements when we made them. I casually walked back to the hotel feeling a bit sad that we hadn't been able to chat. I bought a drink and sat in the bar with my colleagues. Moments later, there was a screeching of brakes followed by loud crashing sound.

We ran outside and saw that a silver sports car had smashed into the phone box, which was completely wrecked. Thankfully, the driver was unhurt and the phone box had been empty at the time. The thought immediately struck me that if Janey had been home and answered the call I would more than likely have been dead. God works in mysterious ways! I had no doubt that he had protected me from yet another disaster.

There had been no guarantee of a full-time job at the end of my apprenticeship, and the company informed me and the other trainees that none of us would be taken on permanently. As I was married and had a mortgage, this was cause for concern. However, we had learned by this time to trust God in all circumstances.

All Things Worked Together for Good

We knew that there was a possibility of me not having a job once the apprenticeship ended. We had already agreed that if that was the case we would move to Devon. Janey's brother was an evangelist and had begun a sort of mission. He held meetings in a barn and lots of people were coming along. We were excited at the prospect of becoming part of the mission.

In order to make the move, I needed a job. Although I had not yet reached the end of my training, I was given time off to look for work. I was offered a job at a small company that did commercial electrical work and repaired electrical motors. We made arrangements to stay at Janey's family home in the short term and travelled down to Devon by train with some basic belongings and tools to start my new job.

I was living in a remote area about ten miles from my new workplace. There was no public transport and the only way I had of getting to work was by hitchhiking – something I had never done before – or walking. Eventually, a regular commuter picked me up and gave me a lift most days. However, sometimes on the way home I would have to walk a long distance before anyone stopped for me.

The supervisor decided to put me in the workshop rewinding motors. I had expected to be out doing installations and repairs, so I wasn't happy about this, but as newly qualified man of twenty I wasn't really in a place to complain. Then when pay day came I had a bit of a shock. I was being paid considerably less than I had as an apprentice at the aluminium smelter. This was disappointing, and I didn't know how we would manage as we were still paying the mortgage on our house in North Wales.

I hated working in the workshop. The work was difficult and they expected a lot from me. They had recently fired a trainee, who had basically been the dogsbody, so they expected me to clean up and make the tea. This was degrading, to say the least. After a few weeks there I made a mistake and broke an expensive test instrument. I was taken aside by the supervisor.

"This isn't working out," he said. "You can finish next week."

I was tired and depressed about the long daily walks, the poor pay and the degradation. I surprised myself by saying, "I'll tell you what, I'll finish right now." I collected up my things and phoned a friend to pick me up with all my tools.

I didn't know what I would do next; however, I had a strange confidence that everything would work out. I saw a job for a maintenance electrician at a quarry at the local job centre that seemed better suited to someone with my training and experience. I sent off an application.

I was offered the use of a van to go up to North Wales so I could pick up more of our belongings. Before we returned, we filled the van with anything we thought might be useful. Mum gave me an old Honda 50 step-through scooter that she no longer used. I managed to get it in the van with everything else. At least I would now have transport.

Soon after arriving back in Devon I heard that I was being called in for an interview at the quarry. The manager was a bit concerned about me being so young but was keen to give me a chance. Phone calls were made to people who offered references, and the manager came back into the room smiling.

All Things Worked Together for Good

"We'll take you on," he said.

I was due to start the following week. Again, the pay was poor in comparison to the aluminium smelter, but the opportunity to work plenty of hours was there, so a reasonable wage could be earned if I put the time in.

I was introduced to the rest of the maintenance team. There were four fitters and me: the sole electrician. One of the fitters was also the supervisor. His name was Martin and he was a friendly, helpful man who showed me the ropes and helped me settle in. I soon got used to my daily commute, riding about twelve miles each way on my Honda 50. It was so much better than hitchhiking and being a dogsbody. Things were looking up.

The mission carried on growing, and week by week more people came along. By this time I was part of the music team and played the bass. Sometimes I would also be asked to share a few words. I wasn't used to public speaking and found myself getting a bit nervous. On occasion I was asked to tell the story of my horrendous bike crash and my miraculous recovery.

As there were so many new believers, a baptism service was arranged. A local church offered its facilities and a number of people, including Janey, were baptised. Each candidate would stand before the microphone and give a short word about why they were being baptised and the whole service was recorded. I was asked to be the technician and to look after the sound equipment. It was great to be part of something that was doing so much to grow God's kingdom.

We became more and more involved, and I was playing the bass at most meetings as well as helping with set-up. We would travel all over the place holding open-air meetings, concerts in theatres, and even taking meetings at a big church in London sometimes. Occasionally, I would get home in the early hours and then have to be at work by 7am.

The job was going well, and I soon settled into the swing of things. There was a lot of complicated machinery and electronics and sometimes the machines would break down, bringing the whole process of stone crushing, washing and grading to a halt. The manager was always keen for us to fix it and get it up and running again. On one occasion a machine stopped, and as a result the whole process backed up. I was called on my two-way radio to get it fixed. I went into the switch room, followed by several other people – foremen, supervisors and operators – all waiting for the new electrician to swing into action and fix it.

I started by opening up the electrical panels. I looked over the rows and rows of relays, switches, fuses and controllers. I hated being watched; it made me feel nervous and uneasy. I couldn't tell them I didn't have a clue what was wrong with it, but the truth was I didn't.

The radio suddenly came alive in my pocket. It was the manager. "What's wrong with it and how long will it be?" he barked at me.

I had to act fast. I said the first thing that came into my head: "It's the spondolex. It'll be about half an hour."

There was no such thing, of course; I had made it up to buy myself some time. Fortunately, I was left to get on with it as my audience gradually left me to my own devices. I found some electrical system drawings and unfolded them on the floor. Without six people breathing down my neck I was able to logically work through it. I soon found the problem and got everything up and running again.

It was time to go home one day but some of the machinery was still running. There was a loud screeching as the drive belts to one of the big stone crushers started slipping. Martin asked me if I would stay on and help him get the jammed machine cleared. I made my excuses and headed off on my scooter. There was a church meeting that night and I didn't want to miss it.

Someone at the meeting said they had heard about an accident at the quarry. It sounded serious. I later heard on the radio that Martin had been killed trying to clear the crusher. A large piece of metal had broken off an excavator bucket and had jammed the jaw crusher. The only way to fix it was to clear the stone and then try to dislodge the metal. The metal had unexpectedly flown out from the jaws under pressure. Martin had been struck by the forty-pound metal part and was fatally injured. His skull was smashed in and there wasn't much anyone could do. He was airlifted to hospital but died soon afterwards. This came as a huge shock to me. I had only been there three weeks and someone was dead.

There were inspectors at the quarry the next day looking at the equipment. A fitter called Steve helped me check the belts and other parts to make sure it was all up to standard. We had to work in the very spot where Martin had died. There was blood spattered all over the motor, and the woolly hat he had always worn under his hard hat lay beside splinters of bone on the floor. It was a horrible scene and we were both close to tears.

I felt so guilty that I hadn't stayed to help Martin. I also realised that it could easily have been me that had been killed. The atmosphere at the quarry was one of stillness and silence. The machines were kept switched off until the safety officers allowed them to be used again.

Sadly, one of the young lads who operated some of the plant machinery died in a car crash a few weeks later. It was a sobering time. These tragic events made me think a lot more about how precious life was, and how fragile we were. I soon realised that it was a dangerous place to work.

On one occasion I was running a cable for some new lighting. Instead of using a scaffold or even a ladder I just climbed over a safety rail and crept along a girder, attaching the cable as I went. There were some big cables on the girder and I had to move one slightly to get my cable in place. As I moved it, there was a big bang and a blinding flash. I couldn't see! The cable had exploded and I was temporarily blinded.

I knew if I fell to the ground there would be broken bones or perhaps worse. I managed to compose myself and hung on. I slowly felt my way along the girder back to the staircase and handrail. I felt my way down the stairs and made my way to the washroom. My left wrist was very sore, and I felt as though I needed to run it under the tap. One of the operators took a look at my wrist and said I needed to go straight to hospital as it looked bad. By the time I got to the washroom my sight was returning. I noticed my wrist was black and badly burned by the flash. As I held it under the cold tap large pieces of skin started peeling off.

All Things Worked Together for Good

I was taken to the nearest A&E department and the waiting room was full. I expected a long wait. The nurse took one look at me and asked if it was an electrical burn. When I said yes I was instantly put on a trolley and taken through to be treated. Thankfully, other than some serious burns I was OK, but I was signed off work for a couple of weeks. This would not be the last time I visited A&E. Either I was working in a dangerous place or I was accident-prone. Or maybe both.

Despite the long hours, hard work and accidents, there also were funny things that happened at the plant. The manager often came to the workshop. He usually wanted to know how long it would take to repair something we were working on. However quickly we did a job he always wanted it done sooner.

One day I tucked a whoopee cushion under my overalls. I stood next to him and squeezed it under my arm.

He turned to me, red-faced with veins bulging in his huge neck, and said: "Don't you ever do that in my presence again! I find that sort of thing disgusting."

He was really angry. I went into my workshop and closed the door. The foreman came in with tears rolling down his cheeks from the laughter.

"He's told me to come in here and give you a good telling off," he said.

Another time I was messing about with the gantry crane in the workshop. I put my arm through the hook and, with the controller in my other hand, hoisted myself up in the air. I was some twenty feet off the floor. The door opened and the manager came in, looking up in the air at me in wonder.

James Ricketts

I promptly took a screwdriver out of my pocket and pretended to do something to the crane.

"It should be OK now. Let me down," I called to my workmates below me.

As soon as I was back on the ground I calmly walked past him and said, "Morning", as if I had been acting perfectly normally. He walked out of the workshop speechless.

One of my duties was to turn the siren on when the men on the quarry face were due to blast. After that, the two-way radios could not be used as they could interfere with the charges. The switch for the siren was in our workshop. At the appointed time I would operate the switch.

On one particular occasion the siren didn't work. I was still very young and inexperienced, so I decided to jump in the Land Rover and drive up to the quarry face to warn them. I could see men in the distance in bright orange overalls, all of whom were waving frantically at me to stop. I stopped and sat there, bracing myself for the explosion. It was probably a hundred yards away, but the massive wall of rock sliding down from the face was dramatic. When the dust settled I was taken to the manager's office and given a good telling off.

Chapter Six

Hiraeth

As time went by and winter drew in, I decided to buy a little car to get about in. I had passed my driving test about a year before but hadn't been able to afford a car. I bought a lime green Austin Allegro for a few hundred pounds. The first time I drove it to Holyhead to visit the family it ran out of oil after a couple of hundred miles. It seemed to have quite an appetite for the stuff.

When we got to Holyhead I decided to investigate. Strangely, there was a sticker on the oil filter with the mileage written on it. "Replaced at 77,000 miles," it read. That was most peculiar, considering that the odometer was only reading 60,000 miles. I found the phone number for the previous owner, who told me the mileage had been over 90,000 when it was sold to the dealer.

James Ricketts

David gave me some legal advice and told me about Trading Standards. When I got back to Devon I rang the dealer. He denied everything and refused to give me any kind of refund. I explained that I had already spoken to the police (this was true, as my brother was a police officer) and Trading Standards, who had asked for his name. He very quickly changed his tune and gave me my money back. Then one of the fitters at the quarry sold me an old Triumph for £50, which served me well for some time.

I began to notice a strange phenomenon. If I was a bit tired and was driving in the evening when it was starting to get dark, I would sometimes see someone step out into the road in front of me. I would slam the brakes on and stop. Sometimes it was on a main road or a dual carriageway. Each time it happened the person looked the same: dressed in a dark tracksuit with dual white lines down the sleeves and legs. Each time I stopped I would jump out of the car, frantically looking for this person I had just run down. There was never anyone there.

Sometimes this would even happen if I was a passenger in someone else's car. I would scream and put my arms up in front of me, as I thought we were going to hit someone. The driver would stop and ask what was wrong, so I would have to explain. It was a scary experience.

I confided in someone about it as it was worrying me. I thought perhaps I was losing my mind. They suggested that perhaps this was some kind of flashback from the motorcycle accident. Perhaps someone had stepped into the road, causing me to swerve. Then maybe the person ran off when they saw what had happened. I guess we will never know. Thankfully, it no longer happens.

All Things Worked Together for Good

It wasn't ideal living at my mother-in-law's house. I was grateful and, as we were still paying for the house in Wales it was helpful. However, we eventually sold the house and had a bit of money left over. I foolishly splashed out on a nice car, but seeing as we were no longer paying the mortgage we were in a position to get a place of our own.

To start with we lived in an old farmhouse, which we rented from the quarry. It was quite big, but it was creepy and Janey didn't like it. She had never learned to drive, so she had to walk a couple of miles to the shops. The walk took her down narrow lanes, which were also used by the quarry trucks. Sometimes when blasting was taking place the whole house would shake and pictures would fall off the walls. There was a large garden and we planned to grow lots of fruit and vegetables. In reality, it was too much for us and we couldn't keep up with all the work. It soon grew into a jungle.

A few months after moving into the farmhouse our first son was born. We called him Philip James. He was blond-haired and blue-eyed. He looked at me not long after I first held him. I thought babies' eyes were closed at first, but he definitely eyeballed me. I was in awe. I was a father for the first time at the age of twenty-one. It was a big responsibility and we were so proud of him. Photos were taken and sent to my parents. They soon came down and stayed at the farmhouse to see their first grandchild. They were understandably besotted with him.

After a few months we took him up to North Wales for a little holiday. Dad worked at a factory where they made prams and kiddies toys, so he was able to get a really nice pram and some lovely toys for his grandson. Philip was already growing fast, with lots of blond hair and chubby cheeks.

It wasn't long before we learned that Philip was to have a brother or sister, and a few weeks before my twenty-third birthday Paul David arrived. By this point we had moved from the farmhouse and bought a newly built house.

I had been getting ready to go to work, and Janey was already up with a bag packed.

"Come on," she said. "Baby's coming."

We drove to the nearby hospital, stopping briefly at a colleague's house to tell him I wouldn't be in that day. Three-quarters of an hour later Paul was born. He was a little smaller than his brother had been at birth. He had thin, wispy blond hair and big blue eyes. I honestly expected the new addition to be a younger version of Philip. We thought they would be like twins with less than a year and a half separating them. We soon learned they were very different in character. In fact, they were like chalk and cheese!

My work at the quarry was sometimes hard going. Sometimes I was needed at work in the early hours and would also have to work late. The manager refused to put me on call, so that meant doing lots of hours. I once calculated that I was working more than ninety hours a week. The only 'weekend' I had was a few hours on a Sunday afternoon. As a result, I didn't see my boys very much when they were first born. They were asleep when I left in the morning and when I came home. Something had to change.

Despite all the overtime, we still had quite a big mortgage and never seemed to have any money. One weekend I travelled up to North wales alone to attend a family wedding. It occurred to me that we could sell our home in Devon and buy a much cheaper property back in my hometown. This would mean I could work 'normal' hours and enjoy a slower-paced life. The prospect of living back in Holyhead excited me.

After returning home, Janey and I talked about the possibility of moving back to Wales. I applied for two jobs: one at a factory that made car parts and another working for the local electricity board. I used my parents' address as I thought employers might be biased against someone applying from England. I was contacted by both companies and interviews were set up. Thankfully, I was able to attend both during the same visit.

The factory interview was quite informal and straightforward. I felt it had gone well. The electricity board interview was rather more formal. I was greeted by a panel of about five men sitting on the other side of a large desk from me. I found it very daunting. I was asked lots of questions; some technical, others about my background and experience.

Then the more senior interviewer asked a very rude question: "I see you're from Holyhead. Do you have any police records?"

I was stunned by this question, and at the same time angered by his arrogance. He had obviously assumed that everyone from my town was a criminal.

I replied: "Yeah, I've got 'Message in a Bottle' and 'Walking on the Moon'." (For those who don't know, these were the song titles of a band called The Police in the 80s. Oh, and records were what we had before iTunes and Spotify!)

I thought to myself, 'I've really blown it now.'

They spoke among themselves rapidly in Welsh and said they would be in touch.

A week or so went by and then the letters arrived: two on the same day. I was working down in the quarry at the time, so Janey rang me at the workshop.

"Which job do you think you got?" she asked.

I had no idea and the suspense was killing me.

"Both of them!" she said.

I was stunned. Why would two employers, both offering good jobs with competitive salaries, want me? Well, that was it. The best job with the least commuting was at the electricity board. I sent off a letter of acceptance and was given a start date. I told my manager at the quarry that I was leaving. He was very disappointed but wrote me a glowing reference.

The house in Devon was sold and we bought a big house in one of the nicest streets in Holyhead. It was a bit old and needed a little work, but it was nothing I couldn't handle. I had already started work three weeks prior to the move and taken the Friday off to drive a van down south to move everything up to our new home. We were living in a beautiful house with sea views and I was working a thirty-seven-hour week instead of ninety. What could be better?

We got involved in the local church. I was on the music team with my bass and did plenty of practical work making improvements to the building. It was hard for Janey with two young boys under the age of three. It was also difficult keeping them quiet during meetings. Paul was a bit hyperactive and always on the go. He could usually be persuaded to cooperate with a continual stream of sweets!

We grew a little concerned that he wasn't speaking. He would just point at things and cry. He would also point at things on his plate and expect to be hand-fed. Phil would try to do things for his little brother and often spoke for him. We thought that perhaps this was why Paul's speech was delayed.

One day, Phil managed to get into the bathroom. Being inquisitive, he wanted to know what was in the various bottles and jars. When we found him he was covered from head to foot in baby powder. We wanted to be cross and tell him off, but we couldn't contain our laughter. He didn't like the fact that we were laughing at him.

A year or so passed by and we were finding things tough. Mortgage rates had gone through the roof and had reached fifteen percent. This meant we were struggling to meet our monthly costs. I had taken out a loan to buy a nice car from someone at work. This had proved to be a rash move as the mortgage was costing so much. But the old car was causing me problems and was unreliable, and as I needed to travel to work every day it had seemed logical to get a decent car.

Things were particularly tough at one point and I really didn't know how we were going to get through the week. We were overdrawn at the bank and maxed out on the credit card. I did the only thing I had left to do: I prayed. People often use this as a last resort, but we really should try doing it as a first option!

The next day there was a knock at the door. It was a work colleague, and he wanted some help with a big job he was doing. A few days later there was money in my hands.

I spent most of my working hours with another local electrician called Spence. He was scruffy, long-haired and into heavy metal. The electricity board sent out leaflets to all the houses in the area advertising its services. We would do things like rewiring houses, putting Economy 7 heating in and installing showers.

The leaflet showed smart-looking workers wearing neat uniforms and ties. They were smiling and clean-shaven and the strapline was 'Call the Experts'. The reality appeared in the form of Spence and myself. I wasn't as scruffy as my colleague, but I was usually unshaven with torn jeans and a grubby T-shirt.

We arrived at a house to install a heating system one day. This meant one of us would need to go up into the attic to pull in the cables.

"Looks like it's your turn," I said to Spence, motioning towards the trap door with my head.

He refused and a small disagreement followed. We ended up rolling around on the floor, scuffling. It was just a laugh really, but perhaps we went too far. The customer, an older lady, soon appeared in the hallway. She started screaming and threatening to call head office and the police. We got up from the floor and apologised. I convinced her we were really good mates and were just messing about, and we promised to do a really good job. So much for calling the experts!

The next job site was quite far away; over an hour's drive in the van. At the end of the day I decided I didn't want to drive on the way back as I had driven there. I jumped in the passenger side, put my seatbelt on and locked the door.

All Things Worked Together for Good

I saw Spence looking at me, trying to think of a plan. He grabbed my lunchbox and threw it across the car park. I had to get out of the van to retrieve it, and by the time I returned he was settled in the passenger seat. I then grabbed all his beloved heavy metal tapes and threw them.

After about an hour things had escalated to the point where we were throwing each other's toolboxes across the car park. What's more, we were going to be late. It was childish behaviour, but we were both laughing our heads off.

"OK, Spence, I'll drive," I reluctantly said.

Things like this happened every day and I enjoyed my job very much. The pay wasn't the best, but what fun we had!

Eventually, we decided to sell the big house. It was too much for us to keep paying for with such high interest rates. We bought a house on the other side of town. It was smaller but had a huge garden.

It needed some rewiring and lots of timber needed replacing. The house was empty and the owner gave me the keys a week before the moving in date, so I set about doing all the necessary work. On moving day I was still putting the floors back down moments before the van arrived with the furniture.

By this time, Paul was three and Phil was going on five. We were still worried about Paul not speaking. At Christmastime, we put the boys' stockings and presents downstairs in the lounge. I remember getting up on Christmas morning and being cross with Phil. He had opened all of Paul's presents for him, thinking he was being helpful. Paul wasn't interested in anything we had bought and just ran around the house like he usually did.

James Ricketts

I was working on a large building project at the local RAF base. The housing estates were being upgraded and it was my job to rewire the houses. The windows had been taken out and had scaffolding around them as we worked on them. There were other tradespeople working alongside us and the plumbers would often leave copper pipes lying around. I thought back to my trumpet-playing days and picked up a length.

I discovered that if I put a reducing fitting on the end it worked like a mouthpiece. I gave it a blow and got a crystal-clear note. I soon found out I could play songs like 'Amazing Grace' on it with relative ease. The plumbers would be rolling on the floor laughing with tears in their eyes. They thought it was so funny. They took the pipe and bent it on a machine, wrapping it round and round and then fitting the top of a hot water cylinder to it, like a French horn. This made it even funnier.

Some of the houses were by a lake. There must have been some rare birds in the vicinity as there were a lot of birdwatchers around. They would stand by the side of the road near the lake, some of them hiding in canvas shelters, many with large lenses. I couldn't resist the urge to get the pipe out. I stuck it out of the window and played 'The Birdie Song' as loudly as I could. The rare birds took flight, while the ornithologists gave me a dirty look, packed up their gear and trudged off.

My younger brother Simon worked at the airbase. He was based there permanently and drove around in a Land Rover or a pickup truck. I had a van, and in those days most cars and vans had petrol engines. We discovered that if you turned the key off and pumped the throttle while driving, the unburned fuel in the exhaust would explode, causing a loud bang.

If Simon saw me he would bang his exhaust, and when I saw him I would bang mine. We thought it was really funny to make a loud bang as we drove past bus stop queues and places where there were unsuspecting victims. People would jump right up into the air at the sound!

One day, a military police officer pulled me over. He had a radio in his hand, and I heard him say, "Yes, it's OK. We've got him now."

I became really worried at this point. Thinking back, we had been quite foolish driving around an MOD base making loud bangs. Due to terrorist activity at the time, most MOD stations were on high alert.

The officer yelled at me: "Is this the van that's backfiring?"

I couldn't really admit to him that I had been doing it on purpose just for kicks.

"Errr, yes it does make a funny noise sometimes," I replied.

The officer still seemed annoyed.

"Well, get it fixed immediately!" he barked.

I felt a bit sheepish as I carefully drove away.

My car broke down and was in serious trouble. The engine had blown and needed a complete rebuild. Apart from this, I couldn't open it up as the keys had mysteriously disappeared. Paul had a habit of throwing things, so we kept asking him where they were. The trouble was, he still didn't speak and wasn't very cooperative. Weeks later I was digging up the garden at the back of the house to lay a patio and there was a 'ching' as the spade hit something. I reached down into the turf and there were my keys.

The car was still in bits by then. Janey had gone into town with the boys, and in the time it took her to come back I had borrowed an engine hoist from a neighbour, taken the engine and gearbox out of the car and completely stripped them down. Oily parts lay around the lounge floor on sheets of newspaper.

For some reason she was cross about this! Not long beforehand I had taken a window out to install patio doors and had used an angle grinder to chop the masonry out. Unfortunately, preparations for these kinds of jobs tend to be low on my priority list. The whole house was thick with dust. I was in the doghouse on that occasion as well!

So we were without a car for a while, but thankfully I had the use of a van for work. Simon also had an old Mitsubishi Colt that he was no longer using.

He rang me up one day and said: "I've had enough of this car. If you can start it, you can have it."

He hadn't been able to start it and had got so annoyed that there was a great big dent in the driver's door where he had given it a decent kicking. Perhaps he had wanted to give it 'a damn good thrashing' like Basil Fawlty did. I like a challenge, so I headed off to my parents' house where Simon still lived.

He had replaced most of the parts within the ignition circuit, but despite having been treated to new plugs, points and high-tension cables it still refused to start. I opened the bonnet and scanned the engine bay. I immediately spotted a loose wire on the ignition coil and popped it back on.

All Things Worked Together for Good

I slammed the bonnet shut confidently and said, "Give me the keys" with a smirk.

The car started easily and purred into life. I wound down the window and said "Bye!" a bit sarcastically. Then I drove off, wheel-spinning down the road. I looked behind me and Simon was standing in the driveway with his jaw hanging open. I felt a bit proud that some of my dad's ability to fix things had rubbed off on me. When I had fixed my car properly I sold the Mitsubishi and gave Simon half the money, but we still joke about it from time to time.

Like me, Simon was an electrician, but he had come to a crossroads in his life after being made redundant. He decided to follow in the footsteps of our other brother David, who had made a successful career for himself in the police force. Simon was in the process of applying and part of the process involved a fitness test. He would be required to run a mile and a half in under twelve minutes. I decided to support him by training with him every day.

We drove away from the house and as soon as the car's odometer showed one-and-a-half miles we stopped, and I sprayed a line of silver paint onto the road. It was a quiet road in the countryside that wasn't used much. Each day we would set off from the house and run to the line.

I had never really been able to run well. When we had done cross country at school I had ended up walking most of the way. Training with someone else makes you more accountable and less likely to back out or give up. Simon was six years my junior and lighter on his feet. He would usually be sitting on the wall holding the stopwatch when I reached to the line, puffing and panting. However, little by little it got easier and we grew faster.

After a few weeks we were both easily beating the police target. Simon was still a bit quicker than me and I could never quite catch him. On one occasion I was determined to beat my personal best and, during the last section, I really gave it everything I had. I sprinted for the finish line painted on the road. As usual, Simon was sitting on the wall, stopwatch in hand.

As I crossed the line I dropped to the ground like an Olympic sprinter, gasping for breath. I was lying on my back with Simon leaning over me, telling me my time. The next moment a car screeched to a halt next to me and people started running towards me. Seeing me lying on my back gasping with someone standing over me, they thought I was having a heart attack and were ready to administer CPR. I thanked them for their concern and explained what had happened. They laughed and went on their way.

Chapter Seven

Back to School

I came home from work one day to find my neighbour in the house holding Paul and fanning him. He had a high temperature. Paul had experienced some kind of seizure and Janey had panicked and gone next door for help. It turned out to be due to the high temperature rather than anything more sinister.

The doctor arrived to examine him. Phil ran into the lounge and out onto the patio through the large patio doors. The problem was, they were closed! Bang! He fell to the floor as he hit the toughened glass. He got up, rubbed his head momentarily and said to the doctor, who looked stunned, "Didn't hurt!" Then he opened the door and ran back into the garden.

James Ricketts

Like his brother, and perhaps more so, Paul seemed to have no fear. He would often go through the hedge and into next door's house. They would find him upstairs looking out of a window into the garden. They would bring him back and were never angry about it, but they were worried he might get out onto the busy road.

At three years old he still had no speech. After he had been put to bed, we would sometimes find him right up at the end of the back garden in his pyjamas. I once climbed a ladder into the attic, which was about ten feet up from floor level. I removed the hatch and climbed in. Moments later, Paul's little face appeared at the hatch. I pulled him to safety. Whenever I fixed the shed roof he would climb up and get on top of the roof with me. We really had to keep an eye on him.

At the age of four Paul was attending my old primary school, as Phil was. Paul was in a preschool unit, but he was already proving to be a handful. Still lacking speech skills, and with a tendency to run off in the opposite direction, he was hard work for the teachers. He escaped from school on more than one occasion and we were politely told that he couldn't continue there.

We were referred to a preschool unit for children with special needs a few miles away in Llangefni, which horrified us. This was a place for children with severe mental and physical conditions, or so we thought. Paul did not fall into that category, so we refused their help at first, but we decided to give it a go after a friend advised us to do so. A taxi would arrive at the house every day to take him to and from the school. He didn't seem to mind and there was more one-to-one help there. He did really well, and his learning and behaviour began to improve.

We still had no idea why he was so different. He certainly had a unique way about him compared with most children. I would sometimes test him if he was eating a packet of sweets. I would wait until he was down to the last sweet and ask him for one. Unlike most children, he would always offer it.

He also seemed fascinated with things like pipes and wanted to know where they went and what they were for. He would look up at the ceiling and point out the location of all the upstairs furniture, as if he had X-ray vision. He created long lines of toys that led down the stairs or from room to room. It was as if he was in a world of his own.

Paul was taken to the local hospital for all manner of tests and a paediatrician examined him. They stuck needles in him to take blood samples and he never complained. When they were finished, He pulled the needle out himself and gave it back to the nurse. None of the tests indicated anything out of the ordinary. Paul had nothing physically wrong with him.

By this point I had become more and more involved with the church. I would sometimes be asked to stand in for the pastor when he was away and would preach on occasion. People told me I had a gift for preaching and I wondered if I was being 'called' to ministry. I put the idea to the back of my mind as it would mean studying at Bible College for several years. How could someone like me with a family to support and bills to pay do such a thing? It seemed impossible.

James Ricketts

We often forget that nothing is impossible with God. He will always find a way, and if it's something He wants for you it will happen if you follow his leading. One Wednesday night at the Bible study meeting I had the distinct impression that God had indeed called me to serve him in some way, so Bible College was the next logical step.

I shared the news with Janey. I expected her to be reluctant to step into unknown territory and the possibility of future hardships with me, but she was as excited as I was. We decided to test the waters and contacted the Elim Bible College in Nantwich (which has since become Regents Theological College in Worcestershire). There was no point in us making plans to go if they didn't think it was right. They invited us to come and have a look around and to meet the principal. This was an anxious time as well as an exciting one.

I expected to get a grilling from the college principal and to be asked why I thought I was being called to such a place as this. I was ready to justify myself, but there was no need. We talked over the practicalities of college life and then went into the office next door to meet the director of studies. He was a Swiss-German man, and it turned out he knew my dad from his Bible college days. This put me at ease. He recommended the Diploma of Higher Education in Theology and Christian Ministry. It would involve two years of full-time study.

As I had done some academic study to get my trade qualifications and some in-depth Bible studying at my church I was allowed to skip the preliminary studies year, which most students are expected to undertake. But there was still the question of finance. How would we afford the fees? Would we get a grant? Would I even be offered a place? It was time to get down to some serious prayer. People told me that if God wanted me there he would make a way.

A week later, the phone call came. I had been offered a place. I was excited, but at the same time I felt worried about the other practicalities. I went to Citizens Advice and asked about getting a grant. I was told that grants for these sorts of courses were 'discretionary' and was shown how to apply. I quickly filled out the forms and sent them off. We put the house on the market and expected a quick sale.

We didn't know where we were going to live or how we would pay for everything at this point, and I even started to doubt my academic ability. I looked at the calendar. The course started in October, so I counted back ten weeks, which is the average time a house sale takes to complete. I declared that if our house hadn't sold by this date we would not be going.

The date came and went, and there was still no sale. We decided to go to Nantwich and look at a few properties there. We walked into an estate agent's and asked for details of all the properties in our price range.

The rather snooty salesman replied, "You won't find anything for that price round here."

I was downhearted, but we continued our search and found three houses that were within our range. The last one seemed ideal. It needed a bit of work, but it was already empty. With a bit of painting and decorating and a new kitchen, it would make an ideal home for us.

Despite not having had a sale on our own house, I made a bold move. Sometimes a step of faith is needed. It's not always enough to say that you believe something; action is needed. God then sees that you mean business and things start happening.

We made an offer and it was accepted by the owner. I was a little worried, but we knew God had the situation under control. A couple of weeks passed. Five weeks before the start of term an offer was made on our house and we set the ball rolling for our big move.

Shortly after this a grant came in. It would cover half of the annual tuition fee and provide a maintenance grant for us to live on. There would be sufficient money left over from the house sale to pay for my half of the two-year fees. All the loose ends were cleared up and finally, at the end of September 1993, we were packed and ready to go. A new adventure awaited us.

Dad offered to drive a van up to Nantwich for us. We hired a big truck and got it loaded up. Janey, the boys and I headed off, and Dad followed us in the truck. We were within about thirty miles of our new home when the car's engine died! I tried everything I could to get it going, but the cam chain had snapped. It couldn't be fixed as a roadside repair and there was no breakdown cover in those days, but Dad was always ready for emergencies like this. He had a piece of rope with him and simply tied the car to the back of the truck. The boys climbed up into the cab with Grandad.

At first Dad drove carefully, but as we continued I think he forgot we were being towed along behind him. Janey was yelling at me to slow down, but I replied that I couldn't, pointing at the tow rope!

There was a place near the college that sold second-hand car parts. We left the car there and were given the number of someone who could fit another engine. It wasn't a great start, but we finally made it to our new home.

The new house was somewhat smaller than the previous one, but it didn't matter to us. We were where we were meant to be, and it was only temporary. We managed without a car for a while as everything was in walking distance. There was an excellent primary school around the corner and we soon learned this was where most of our fellow students sent their children.

Despite Paul's difficulties he was placed in a mainstream class with a teacher aid, who gave him one-to-one help. Phil fitted right in and soon made friends. Everything seemed to be slotting into place.

I headed off to college for the first day of orientation, briefcase in hand. It felt strange to be a student again after all that time. I soon learned there were many other mature students in my year. We were given our timetables and shown around the college campus and facilities.

Most of the students lived on campus, either in rooms or in self-contained flats. We soon got to know people and made some good friends. For some reason, most of my friends were either Irish, African or Indian.

We were also expected to take part in several hours of practical work around the college each week. Some worked in the kitchens, others cleaned rooms and made beds, and some did gardening. Others, like me, had specific and useful skills. I was placed with the college handyman to do electrical work around the campus. It was a good way of 'keeping my hand in'.

One of Paul's difficulties was that he simply couldn't sit at a table to be taught. Within seconds he would be up out of his seat and running around. We were called into the school as Paul's teacher wanted to see us. We went into the classroom and there was Paul standing in a queue with his book, waiting to see the teacher. We thought this was amazing. She then told us something funny. Paul had been up at her desk, and after she had finished talking to him she had said: "OK, Paul. Hop back to your desk."

And this is literally what he had done. He had hopped backwards to his desk on one leg, then sat down. She soon learned that Paul took everything literally. We had to be extra careful at mealtimes. If we said, "Paul, can you chuck me the potatoes?" or, "Throw me the salt," he would quite literally do so. But overall we were really pleased with the progress our boys were making.

Part of the college course involved a church placement. Our first assignment was with a small church of about ten to fifteen folk who met in a rented room. I was a little disappointed as I had been expecting a larger church so close to a big city. We went along every week, and I would be asked to preach and lead sometimes. I would be given constructive criticism by the pastor afterwards.

Shortly after this, I was asked to take a group of students to a bigger church in Manchester as I had a car and there had been transport problems getting other students to their placements. I agreed to go, but this meant being away from the church every Sunday and leaving Janey and the boys behind. They continued to go along to the local church.

All Things Worked Together for Good

This team of students and I would drive up to Manchester and go to the morning service. We would have lunch with a different church member or family every week. In the afternoons the pastor would give us insights into ministry life, look at sermons we were planning to preach and give us advice and help.

One week we were having lunch with a lady from the church. The potatoes were a bit on the hard side. Most of the team just ate the food, but one man, a plain-speaking Yorkshireman, spat out the food and exclaimed, "These potatoes aren't cooked!" I cringed as the lady apologised.

As we always arrived back quite late from the evening meetings, the students in my team who lived on campus missed their evening meals. Janey offered to cook a meal every Sunday night so we enjoyed a nice meal together and talked about the events of the day.

The academic side of the course was demanding. Everything had to be typed, double-spaced and well presented, and sources had to be documented in the footnotes. I was a hands-on kind of guy and wasn't really used to this. I would type my work out and my sentences were always really long. I wasn't sure how and where to use paragraphs, and my general grammar was lacking. Thankfully, Janey had been trained as a secretary and knew her way around a keyboard, so I soon learned how to present my work.

Time management wasn't a skill I possessed, so I usually ended up burning the midnight oil to finish research papers, handing them in right on the deadline. But overall, I seemed to be doing quite well.

James Ricketts

Chapter Eight

New Horizons

Because I was applying to enter the ministry, I was required to do what is known as a 'three-week mission'. This involved working alongside a senior church minister at one of the larger churches, so I was sent off to a large church in Scotland. To me, this was like going abroad.

I set off on the long journey. I heard there were roadworks on the motorway, so I made a detour. I was at a roundabout when a car hit me quite hard at the front on the left-hand side. I motioned to a layby up the road and we exchanged details. My car was wrecked, but I figured it was still driveable with a few adjustments. The other driver had apologised, so I assumed he was accepting blame. He later denied everything and claimed I had hit him!

I managed to find a piece of rope to tie the bumper back on. Sticky tape and polythene were used to temporarily fix the broken headlight. I got back on the road and headed north. I also had some problems finding the house where I was meeting the pastor. I stopped many times and asked for directions, but it was hard to understand what was being said. Eventually, after many hours of driving, writing my car off and getting lost, I arrived. I was welcomed in, given a hasty meal and then we were off out to a youth meeting.

I was introduced to the youth group and asked to give a short talk. After the meeting I was taken to a house where I was to be accommodated for the next three weeks. A nice family welcomed me into their home and we soon became good friends. The church was in Glasgow, which was a big city. I wasn't really used to driving in cities, so I was understandably a bit nervous.

I was told to report to the church offices the following week. The pastor was most insistent that I wore a shirt and tie. I preferred the casual look myself, and on one occasion I was sent back to the house to change!

I was given a list of names and addresses for people who were members of the church or had attended at some time. "Go and visit them," I was told.

I set off on foot to begin with, as many of the addresses were near the church office. I was getting strange looks. Someone told me that because I was wearing a suit people thought I was either police or the Department for Work and Pensions (DWP), so they were naturally wary of me.

On one occasion I heard someone cry out, "Hey you!" I ignored it and carried on walking. The shout came again. This time, I could hear the quick movement of feet, as whoever it was clearly wanted to get my attention. I waited for the knife in my back or a blow to the head.

"Excuse me, pal," he said in a thick Glaswegian accent. "Your shoelace is undone."

There I was nervously expecting the worst, and this person was merely concerned that I might trip over.

I went from house to house to see the people on the list. At first I was worried. What would we talk about? Would it be awkward? I soon learned that the people I encountered were the kindest and most open I had ever met. Very soon after meeting them they would tell me their life stories, and they invariably gave me food and drink. We would talk openly about anything that was troubling them and then pray together. I soon realised there was a lot more to 'the ministry' than holding meetings on a Sunday and preaching.

I visited people in hospital, prison and drug rehabilitation units. I found I was being worked really hard, and it gave me an appreciation for the work that goes on in pastoral ministry. At the end of each day I would return to my host's home for a quick meal and then I was usually off out again for more church activities. It was a very busy time.

I was given one day off each week. On my first day off, some of the youth offered to take me out and show me the sights. We drove a long way to visit Loch Lomond and several other places of beauty. Then we went to a Chinese restaurant and shared a meal. The youth members quickly disappeared after the meal, so I went to the counter to pay thinking I had been left to pick up the bill. The man behind the counter explained that it had been paid in full.

Janey and the boys came up by train for my last week. She hadn't been well and being so far away I had been worried. I met them at the railway station and we went back to the house where I was staying. We had a great day out on my last day off, travelling around the countryside. All too soon it was time to return to college. A few weeks later it would be time to start my next year of study.

For as long as I can remember I had dreamed of visiting a faraway land. I don't know why, but the thought of travelling to a distant country fascinated me. Something significant happened at the beginning of the following year. After spending some time in prayer I had a sense that something would be very different that year.

I can't remember all the details, but Janey and I both became aware of a particular country that seemed to be drawing us for some reason. Everywhere we looked, we seemed to see something about New Zealand. One day, Janey spelled it out: "I think we're meant to go to New Zealand."

We had always said we would go wherever God called us and had never really had any idea what would happen after my college course finished.

I confidently declared: "If this is God, we'll go there this year to see for ourselves."

This was a bold statement. We had no money and no obvious way of getting the several thousand pounds together that we would need for tickets, accommodation and other travel costs. We didn't even have passports as we had never ventured out of the country.

As I said in a previous chapter, we sometimes we have to take steps of faith in order to set things in motion. We may need to demonstrate to God that we are serious about a particular issue. We immediately went to the post office, had photos taken and applied for our passports. Things were starting to get real. We knew there was going to be a major shift that year.

I was halfway through my second year of study and things were going well. I wasn't a grade-A student, that was certain, and I preferred socialising to sitting in the library every night with my head in a book, but I was holding my own.

One day I was called into the administrator's office as the lady who did the accounts wanted to talk to me. She seemed excited.

"You won't believe it," she said, "but your education authority is the only one in the country that has decided to start paying course fees in full."

I did believe it! God had a habit of turning situations around when we least expected it. As I had already paid for the full two years upfront, I was due a refund from the college. I did a few sums in my head and realised I was a third of the way towards finding the money we needed for our New Zealand trip.

I don't know why, but I must have considered the possibility of continuing my studies for a third year. As soon as I was handed the cheque, I remembered saying: "If God wants me to do another year of study the fees will be paid in full."

As my second-year grades had been reasonable, there would be no problem continuing my studies to degree level. So that was it. We would head off to New Zealand for a month in the summer, then back to college for another year of study. I had mixed feelings, but I was excited.

We prayed and prayed that God would provide the rest of the money we needed. I think we expected an envelope to land on the doormat one day with the exact amount we needed in it. It's not unheard of, after all.

I was thinking about that 'miracle envelope' while looking out of the window one day and my gaze was drawn to my car. It wasn't a fantastic car, but it was still worth a bit. I heard a voice saying, "It doesn't always work like that, James." It wasn't an audible voice, but in my spirit I knew that God was speaking and all thoughts of miracle envelopes evaporated. I knew, without a doubt, that the car had to go.

I put the car up for sale in the local paper and started looking for a cheaper one. I found one for a hundred and fifty pounds. It was already taxed and tested, so I knew that it was in a reasonable condition. A week or two went by and I was stuck with two cars, so I started to doubt my judgement. But then I received a phone call a few days later from someone who wanted to look at my car. I was asking for a thousand pounds. I have bought and sold a lot of cars in my time and one thing is for sure: the buyer will always try to knock the price down and make offers.

The potential buyer arrived at the house. I showed him the car, he drove it round the block and then he asked me how much I wanted for it.

"I want a thousand pounds," I replied.

"Here you go, then," he said.

He handed me the exact amount. There was no haggling and no fuss; just another chunk towards the big trip.

All Things Worked Together for Good

That summer we went to the church's annual conference at a holiday resort. One of the main speakers was from New Zealand and we managed to get a meeting with him. We told him how we felt about our call to his country. He asked for our details and I gave him a CV. He said he would arrange an itinerary of preaching appointments and places for us to stay around the country. This was amazing! We had no idea what we wanted to do or where we should go when we got there, so it felt as though God was taking care of all the details.

A few weeks later, a friend came to visit. He was about to trade in his car for a nearly new one. It was one of those deals where it didn't matter what was traded in there would be a fixed part-exchange amount towards the new one. He was also looking for a sofa and we had one he liked. We ended up doing a deal where we swapped our old banger for his car, which was a bit newer, and threw in the sofa just to sweeten the deal. He drove away in my old car with the sofa strapped to the roof rack.

The boys loved the new car. It was a sporty hatchback with lots of gadgets. It even had a CB radio and a big, long whip aerial. It also had a really good stereo. I pulled the stereo out and sold that for £100 by itself. After a while I got to thinking and decided to sell the newer car as well. It would be more money in the account, which contained almost the amount we needed.

I had resigned myself to the idea of having no car, but another student had upgraded and decided to give me his old one. It needed a bit of work, but nothing that was beyond me. We were amazed! Now there was no doubt. We were going! The trip was on.

James Ricketts

Our plane tickets were booked and we decided to reserve a hotel room for our first night in New Zealand. The rest of the time we would be staying with people from the churches we visited or at backpacker lodges and B&Bs.

To start with we thought we would all be going. We had included our sons in the plans. However, the more we thought about it the more we realised that it would be difficult to bring them. I didn't want to disappoint them, but we needed to see how they felt about staying behind while we went on our own.

I asked them if they would like to stay with Grandma and Grandad for the summer while we went to New Zealand. We expected them to be upset about the thought of staying behind, but they were really pleased and excited at the prospect of spending the summer with their grandparents. This was a big relief for us.

The day before we were due to fly out, we were all set to drive the boys to my parents' house in Holyhead. We only got a few miles down the road before the car started misfiring badly. This was the car I had been given by my fellow student the month before. It wasn't looking good. What could I do? I drove back to town with the car spluttering. By this point the boys were upset and close to tears, thinking their holiday plans were scuppered. I reassured them that everything would be all right.

I drove to the house of a good friend, Ben, who was in the same class as me at college. He was from Zambia and lived nearby with his wife and two children. It was early on a Sunday morning. I knew they travelled to a church about twenty miles away and would need their car, but I didn't know what else to do. I explained the situation and he offered me his car without hesitation. I told him I would return it the next day.

I had a reputation among the other students for my knowledge of cars, so people would often bring theirs round for me to fix. Sometimes they would ask me to check over a car they were thinking of buying.

A few months previously Ben had asked me to have a look at this particular car, as he was thinking of buying it. It was a large saloon car with a big engine and an automatic gearbox. I remember climbing into the driving seat with Ben sitting beside me. I had put the car through its paces and driven it fast, screeching around bends and accelerating away from junctions.

Ben had gone completely quiet, so I asked if he had already taken it for a test drive.

"Yes," he had replied, his eyes wide with terror, "but not like this."

The day finally arrived for our big trip. A friend took us by car to Stoke-on-Trent, and we caught a bus to Heathrow from there. A couple of hours later we arrived at the airport. We were both a bit nervous about the flight as neither of us had flown before and we were about to embark on a twenty-eight-hour trip!

As we stood in the queue, a lady from the airline was walking down the line asking if anyone was willing to fly out the next day as the flight was overbooked. She was offering a financial incentive and a free night in a hotel, so we said yes.

This meant we were kept on standby until we knew what was happening with our original flight, so we didn't check in our bags right away. We were given a voucher for free food and drink, which took our minds off things and made us feel a bit more relaxed. We wouldn't know until the flight was ready to leave whether we would be getting on it or not.

As it happened, some people hadn't shown up, so there was space for us. Our bags were checked in and we were hurried towards the exit gate. We found ourselves sitting on the plane, waiting for take-off. The engines revved up to speed and the plane hurtled down the runway. I could tell that Janey was nervous and she gripped my hand tightly.

As soon as we were up to cruising altitude I went for a walk around the plane. We were in middle-aisle seats, so there was no window near us. I stood beside the exit for ages looking down at the tiny houses and roads below us. There was also a display on the back of the seat that showed a real-time map of our position. It seemed to move very slowly. When we finally reached the Pacific Ocean the whole screen turned completely blue, with no land mass in sight.

We finally landed in Auckland and took a shuttle bus to the hotel we had pre-booked. Janey just wanted to sleep, but I was too excited. I wanted to get out and explore! We rested for a while and then I went down to the city to pick up the hire car before returning to the hotel. It was mid-summer back home and mid-winter in New Zealand, although it didn't feel like it. The air was warm and the sky was cloudless.

We awoke quite early the next morning and headed up north. Our itinerary gave us a few days to get to Whangarei on the north-eastern coast. We had budgeted a daily amount for food and travel, so we knew we had to be quite careful. We worked our way up the east coast, exploring all kinds of towns, forests and beaches. A lot of the roads were just gravel tracks, which amazed me. The scenery was amazing, with palm trees and ferns everywhere.

We stayed at a B&B the first night, then at backpackers' lodges, which were great. A private room with bed linen was provided, along with communal facilities and a kitchen. Although there were facilities to cook our own meals, we soon worked out that it was cheaper to eat out.

We arrived at our first appointment within a few days of our arrival. We had been sent to the home of a family from the church who had kindly offered to put us up. The church was quite a big one. They hadn't invited me to preach, probably because they had never heard of me and church leaders need to be careful who they allow into their pulpits! But we were welcomed by the church and invited to share a few words about who we were and why we were in New Zealand.

We moved on after a couple of days and headed for the Bay of Islands. As it was off-season most of the motor camps were empty, but a chalet could be rented for a reduced price. We decided to travel from there right to the top of the country, which consisted of a long, narrow peninsula. A small car and mainly gravel roads made the travelling a bit tiring. We made it a day or two later and were amazed to find a beach that was ninety miles long.

We spent a month travelling around like the country. We had been given an appointment to meet with the 'top brass' of the Elim movement in New Zealand. We had attended similar meetings with executive church leaders before, so we dressed accordingly. I wore a shirt, tie and smart suit.

Janey put her best clothes on and we sat in the lobby waiting to be called in.

A barefooted man in shorts and a casual shirt came out to greet us and led us into a room where the rest of the team was waiting to meet us. I was a little surprised that everyone was casually dressed like the man who had greeted us. It seemed things were much less formal in New Zealand, and that suited me just fine.

It was a very relaxed and informal meeting with plenty of laughing and joking. I had sent a VHS tape of one of my preaching appointments ahead of the meeting at their request. They said that they liked my style, but that there were plenty of people who could preach in New Zealand. Nevertheless, we were invited to join Elim New Zealand the following year once my studies were finished. I was warned that there were no guarantees of a ministry appointment and that I would have to find work to start with. I had no problem with this as I was a qualified electrician, and I knew trades like this were in demand there.

We had been invited to speak at a church in West Auckland, and we met a couple there who soon became great friends of ours. Mark had just completed the New Zealand equivalent of the training I was doing, and Nikki was originally from England. We had plenty to talk about and they gave us their phone number. They also offered to put us up if we ever needed somewhere to stay.

There was another family we knew through a church near the Bible College in Nantwich. We heard they had emigrated to New Zealand a year earlier. We had written to them and told them about our upcoming adventure. We just wanted to be in contact with people in a similar situation.

All Things Worked Together for Good

They invited us to stay at their house for a week, which was right out in the bush. It was really nice to be able to talk about the practical aspects of moving halfway around the world. They were really hospitable, taking us out for meals and showing us the sights.

During our travels we visited a place called Napier and the nearby town of Hastings. Since Janey had been born in Hastings, UK, it was fun taking her picture under the sign. Napier had been flattened by a massive earthquake in 1931. As everything had been rebuilt soon afterwards, most of the architecture was in the art deco style. By this time we knew the routine, so we booked into a backpackers' hostel nearby.

We ventured out for a walk around the city that evening. We stopped outside a church and read the noticeboard. As we were doing so, a man came out and asked me who I was. I explained who we were and why we were visiting, and he said, "I want you to come in and talk to these people."

I thought this was a bit strange, but we followed him into the building. The place was full of Maori people and I spent some time talking to them about faith. I was used to preparing my talks beforehand and having notes to keep myself on track, but everything was off the cuff at this church. We spent time with the congregation afterwards, praying for anyone who wanted us to pray with them. We felt humbled and excited at the same time.

Our next appointment was further south in a place called Palmerston North. It was quite a drive, but we took in some amazing scenery on the way. The pastor welcomed us and showed us around the city. We were staying in a kind of outhouse in his garden. The problem was, the toilets were in the main building, which was locked during the night. In the mornings we had to jump in the car and drive to a café to use the toilets and get a cup of tea!

The next day, we were faced with the very long drive back to Auckland. This involved travelling up the main highway through the country. We expected to find a motorway, but it was just a main road. We travelled hundreds of kilometres through really remote areas and saw hardly any other cars on this road. There were long stretches without fuel stations, so we had to make sure we filled up whenever we could.

After the long, tiring drive, we found ourselves back in Auckland. We decided to stay overnight at a motor camp on the North Shore. I phoned Mark and Nikki, who we had met the previous week at the church. They were disappointed that we hadn't called them first as we could have stayed with them. As we had already paid for the night, we invited them over for tea and had a good chat. They invited us to come to their house the next day and we stayed there for the last couple of days before we were due to fly back.

We spent our last day with a senior member of Elim. There was a very large church there with lots of space and plenty of activities going on. It even had its own school. In the evening we shared a meal with our hosts before saying our last goodbyes and being driven back to the airport to prepare for our long return flight.

We returned home quite exhausted. What an adventure! But it had felt as though something was definitely missing: our two blond-haired bundles of energy. We had exchanged a few letters and spoken on the phone whenever we could.

All Things Worked Together for Good

All the same, we had really missed them and were looking forward to seeing our boys again. Dad agreed to bring them home the next day.

We had been away for the whole month of August, mainly because this was really the only time we could be away with it being the summer break from college and the boys' school. There had been a real heatwave in the UK and they had enjoyed some fantastic weather.

I heard the car pull up, quickly followed by rapid footsteps coming towards the house. I opened the door and was greeted enthusiastically by my mega-excited sons. They had so many stories to tell, and so did we. They had obviously spent lots of time outside as they were really tanned and their hair was bleached completely blond.

They excitedly told us of their adventures and it sounded as though they had had a fantastic time. They had been taken on long mountain walks in Snowdonia and Paul had learned to ride his bike at last. He had been riding it at the nature reserve one day when the training wheels had fallen off. He hadn't even noticed, and Grandad had to tell him he was actually riding the bike for himself.

Many a lazy afternoon had been spent at the beach. Grandad knew of some private beaches off the beaten track and away from all the holidaymakers. Tales were told of big sandcastles and deep sand holes they had dug.

We had brought back lots of sweets and chocolates from New Zealand; the sort you couldn't get at home. It had been an amazing month, but it was good to be home.

James Ricketts

Chapter Nine

A New Life Down Under

The new term started and it was time to knuckle down to my studies. Every year the level of expectation on the student increased. The tests were harder, and the assignments grew longer and more complex. As I was doing a degree, I had opted to do an honours thesis. This meant less time in class, with more time researching and reading.

Because of our interest in New Zealand and the many books and newspaper articles I had collected, it struck me that I could do something that would also enable me to find out more about the country and the people with whom we now had a strong connection.

I discussed my plans with the lecturer and he agreed that it was a good idea. Best of all, because this was before the days of the internet and most of my content was from a country on the other side of the world, no one could really argue with the content of my thesis! I lost some marks for grammar but gained a good result overall.

I was very busy during my last year, and organisation and time management weren't my strong points. Assignments would be set at the start of term and the majority of students would start them right away. Not me! I would wait until the night before. Then I would work into the early hours with books all around me, frantically typing away. I would get up early the following morning, edit the paper, then print it out and hand it in just in time, with the ink barely dry.

Christmas break was soon upon us and we had big decisions to make. Following the experience of our summer in New Zealand, we knew there was to be a big move ahead. But how? Getting a visa to live and work permanently in New Zealand would be no easy task. The paperwork was a minefield and would take months to complete.

I contacted a migration consultancy and our position was assessed. Points were awarded for age, professional or trade qualifications, years of work experience, money, family sponsorship and job offers. The good news was that we had enough points, but there was a snag. I needed a job offer.

Over the next few months, papers were sent back and forth from London. We had to obtain medicals, X-rays, certificates and references. At the same time, we put our house on the market and started thinking about where we would live in the interim. The college very kindly offered to let us live in a two-bedroom flat in the main building, giving us a good deal on rent as well as meals in the main canteen. A few weeks later we sold the house and moved into the college flat.

Life on campus was great fun. I loved to socialise, and was always chatting and drinking tea with other students. There was a considerable amount of work to be done before the course finished and I approached it in my usual casual manner.

By this time, my younger brother Simon was also a student at the college. Having two of us on campus was a challenge for the lecturers. However, we were in serious demand from the maintenance team as we were both electricians, so we would carry out repairs and improvements. A big accommodation block was being converted from single rooms into self-contained flats. We were paid a flat rate, which wasn't exactly on a par with the trade, but it meant we were able to save some money.

Simon and I were working on a flat one day and there was also a painter working there who had his radio cranked up really loud. I asked politely if he would turn it down. He refused and turned it up even louder. I walked over to the nearby switch room, unlocked the door and threw the big switch, turning off the electricity for the entire building. We had peace and quiet at last.

When he protested, I told him bluntly: "Don't mess with sparks!"

The last semester finally came to an end. The studies were over but there was still plenty of work to do around the college. Janey also had some paid work, cleaning the nursery. It was handy for both of us to be working on site and for the boys to have a safe environment in which to play and explore, with lots of friends of around their ages nearby.

Visa progress was still painfully slow, with papers and forms continually going back and forth. More questions were asked and more certificates were required. The final requirement was a job offer, which would give us the points we desperately needed. I made lots of enquiries. The contacts we had in New Zealand sent me some details, but no one was really interested until I was ready to show my face over there. It was a stressful time.

Then one day someone sent me the local paper from a suburb of Auckland. There was an advert from an electrical contractor on the back page. The contractor wasn't looking for workers – he was just advertising his business – but I took the number down and waited for the right time to call, bearing in mind the significant time difference.

He sounded enthusiastic on the phone and offered me a job based on the information I had given him. There was no interview, he just asked, "When can you start?" It seemed that good electricians were in demand. This was another major hurdle we had overcome. I explained my visa requirements and he seemed quite relaxed about it.

The weeks flew by, and goodbyes were said to all the students from my year. Some had been offered places at churches around the country. Some would go into teaching, while others went back to their home churches to serve.

It felt strange to still be on campus with everyone gone, but the college was glad to keep us there as was still plenty of work to be done. We had to vacate the nice flat to make way for new students, but I did a deal with the college that allowed us to live in one of the new flats rent-free. There was a catch, though! I was to rewire it for free, as it needed upgrading. Still, it sounded like a good deal and I accepted.

    I started to feel uneasy about the visa situation shortly after this. Letters were not being answered and phone calls were not being returned. A friend of mine was going to London and I asked if I could tag along. I took all the relevant paperwork and our passports along just in case they were needed.

    I found my way across London to New Zealand House and asked to see the lady who was dealing with our case. She came to meet me with a disappointed look on her face.

    "I'm sorry, but we still haven't had your job offer through," she said.

    I explained about the urgency of the situation, and how we had sold our house and everything. We had even sent some of our belongings on ahead as we had been so confident. She felt I had been foolish and that we should have waited until after the decision was made. I sent a fax to my prospective employer, asking him to contact the immigration service, but with the time difference I knew it would be at least a day before I heard anything. I travelled back to the college with a heavy heart and began to doubt whether we were doing the right thing after all.

    I explained the situation to Janey and the boys. We had set a date for our departure and had even booked our flights. The date had come and gone. Thankfully, we didn't lose our flights as they could easily be rescheduled, but the boys were upset when the planned day came and went without the arrival of our visas.

The next morning I'd had enough. All the months of planning and hard work had been for nothing, or so it seemed. I locked myself in the bedroom and gave God an ultimatum. I had even begun to think about forgetting the whole thing and going back to Holyhead. I lay on the bed with months of pent-up emotion boiling over. I was angry and could take no more.

Janey, on the other hand, took a different approach. She remained positive. She put on some Christian worship music and began to sing along, thanking and praising God. Happy and singing, I knew she had something that I was lacking at this point: faith.

About an hour later the phone rang, and I ran to answer it in anticipation. It was New Zealand House. The lady I had spoken to the day before told me that everything was in place and I could return with our passports and sort everything out. It was close to midday by this point. I thought about going the following day, but I decided to race down to Crewe and just jump on a train.

A couple of hours later I was handing over the passports and forms. The words "Welcome to New Zealand" were like music to my ears.

I walked out of the office with a massive grin on my face and found the nearest phone box so I could share the good news. Word soon got out back at the college. Our situation was well known and lots of people had been praying about it. I was met with smiling faces, handshakes and congratulations on my return. This was it! The flights were booked and our plans were made. Parties were laid on for us to say goodbye, but it still didn't seem real. We were about to travel to the other side of the world and live there!

All Things Worked Together for Good

The next day I collected my mail from reception as I usually did. There was a letter from the migration consultants we had used to apply for our permanent residency visas. I opened it up. To my surprise, the envelope contained all the personal papers and certificates we had sent them over the past few months. The letter basically told me the consultancy business was going into liquidation and that they could no longer handle my case. I was amazed at this. Had I not reacted to what my spirit was telling me and rushed down to London, we might never have been able to get the visas sorted out.

We spent a few days with Mum and Dad in Holyhead before we were due to leave. It was a sobering time. We really didn't know when we would see them next. I heard that Dad had said to someone, "We'll never see them again," and that thought saddened me. I didn't want any tearful goodbyes at the airport, so we decided to say our goodbyes in Holyhead and head back to the college for our last day.

Dad was always a bit sentimental. He handed me something before we left. It was a fifty pence piece, sawn in half with a hole in the edge.

"Put it on your keyring, and every time you look at it, think of me and pray," he said.

The coin was dated 1982; the year I had almost died of my injuries after the motorcycle accident. He put the other half of the coin on his keyring and told me he had been using it in the same way every time he looked at it, and would continue to do so.

A friend of mine at college had a big car and we got everything packed into it and ready to go. The back of the car was full right up to the roof and the roof rack was also fully loaded up. Another student offered to come down and wave us off, which was handy as that meant there was enough space for all our things and family members!

A couple of hours later we arrived at Heathrow with our passports, visas and tickets. We were ready to go. Our flight wasn't until about midnight, so we had time to relax with our friends over a coffee. All our bags were checked in, so we only had our hand luggage. To keep costs down my hand luggage was packed full of tools: spanners, screwdrivers, pliers, saws and hammers. I cannot imagine what would happen today if anyone tried to get on a plane with items like that!

We took the four middle seats on the plane so we would all be sitting together. Janey and I took the outer seats and the boys were in the middle. They were so excited! I had explained what would happen during take-off and was worried they would be nervous.

Finally, the engines roared into life and we started hurtling down the runway. The nose of the plane raised and then we were up in the air. I turned to Phil, who was sitting next to me, and asked if he was OK. All I got was "Awesome!"

Paul had always been interested in technical things, so he was too busy taking everything in to worry about anything. I had bought second-hand Gameboys to keep them amused during the flight, but only gave them out when we were aboard. To my surprise, the same games were available on the screens on the back of the seats in front anyway.

I tried to sleep, but Phil stayed awake the whole time watching movie after movie and playing games. After a quick change of aircraft in Singapore we were on the final leg of the journey. As I looked out of the window, it suddenly started getting real. Where would we live? How would I get on in my new job? There was so much going on in my mind.

We soon touched down in Auckland and made it through customs and immigration. David and Claire, the couple we had first met out in the remote suburb, had offered to pick us up from the airport and put us up for a while until we got sorted. Mark and Nikki had just built a new house on the North Shore and had also offered to put us up, but as they were away for a few days we had arranged to go and stay with them about a week later.

James Ricketts

Chapter Ten

The Ups and Downs of Life in Paradise

At last we had arrived. We had reached our destiny. But there was a lot to do. I went to visit the man who had agreed to employ me. He lived right over the other side of the city. He showed me some of the work he had been doing, which was mainly domestic.

This was nothing new to me as I was used to wiring houses. However, New Zealand had its own codes of practice and regulations. Technically, I couldn't work as an electrician until I was registered, but I couldn't get registered unless I was working. It was a catch-22 situation. We agreed a start date and a basic wage, and I was technically an electrician's mate until the paperwork was done.

James Ricketts

To start with, I commuted from the house on the North Shore, but it soon became apparent that we needed to move nearer to my place of work. There was a small town on the outskirts of the East Auckland suburbs that seemed to suit us. It even had a beach. We soon found a house to rent and a school for the boys. We spoke to the head teacher about Paul's special needs and were assured that he would be looked after.

The followed week we made the move. We contacted the removals company to deliver the belongings we had sent over months earlier. In reality, these belongings consisted of nothing more than about a dozen tea-chest-sized boxes containing some clothes, books, kitchen items, bedding and personal possessions. When we finally moved in, all we had besides these items was a fridge, a desk and some beds. The only furniture we had in our lounge was a single large cushion. This was the reality for us at the time. But we were coming into the summer months with cicadas humming in the garden and nice warm air surrounding us. We thought of our family back home facing the ice and snow.

My job was tiring. I always arrived early for work, as has been my way throughout my career. It was about a twenty-kilometre drive to the depot. Even though I wasn't due to start work for fifteen minutes or so, I would be asked to load the van up and get everything ready. There was no morning tea break and we worked solidly until lunchtime. A quick sandwich and bottle of water later and then we worked right up until five o'clock. By the time I got home all I could do was slump into a chair. Phil would want to jump on me and play, but I was exhausted. I have to say that Janey and my boys kept me going in that job. They made it feel worthwhile when I came home at night.

After a week or so in New Zealand we became worried about the boys. They were listless, lacking in energy and struggling to breathe. It was very worrying. They would just lie on the floor a lot of the time. They usually had unlimited energy and were always on the go. It was most unlike them.

When you're in a strange country, it's difficult to know where to turn in these situations. Janey phoned our friends in West Auckland and they told us to take the boys straight to the emergency department in Howick, about twenty kilometres away. We set off straightaway. The boys were put on nebulisers and quickly began to stabilise. After their treatment, we were handed a bill for three hundred New Zealand dollars. This was a shock as we had never had to pay for healthcare before.

Questions needed to be asked about the cause of what turned out to be asthma attacks. Janey discovered that the underlay in every room was made from horsehair. We couldn't be certain if this was the cause, but we pulled every single carpet up, removed it and put it all in the shed at the bottom of the garden. As we were pulling out the underlay, we found a flattened Gecko under the carpet. I don't know if the underlay was the main cause, but the boy's health improved soon after we got rid of it.

We had been asked to work with a small church in another part of the city. We weren't sure what we would be doing there, but were soon welcomed in and put to good use. I was asked to preach and lead small groups, as well as playing in the band. It wasn't exactly how we had envisaged our ministry, but it was a nice community church and we were getting to know some great people.

There was a couple in the church who seemed to like us, and we also enjoyed their company. They often invited us over for barbeques, to have a swim, to laze about in the hot tub, or just to hang out. They were also very kind to us, always giving us things we needed. As we had very few friends in the country and no family around us, this couple was a real godsend.

Financially, things were tough. There were no more family allowance payments, no income tax thresholds and no tax credits. On top of this, Janey and I realised we both needed health insurance. I soon discovered that I wasn't being paid very much. Every week there was a shortfall between the amount of money we had coming in and the amount we needed to pay the bills, put food on the table and fill up the car. We had some money put by, but we were dipping into it every week.

One day, just a few weeks before Christmas, my boss casually announced that he was finishing work the following week and wouldn't be back until February. I stopped and tried to process that in my mind. That was about six or seven weeks off. In Britain it's fairly normal to have two weeks off at Christmas. In New Zealand, the Christmas break is also the start of the summer holidays.

I asked him, "What am I going to do?"

He just shrugged his shoulders and walked away.

This was the last straw as far as I was concerned. A week or so before this he had taken me to a church hall to repair some lighting. The ceiling was eighteen feet or so high. The lights had heavy wire cages over them as the hall was sometimes used for indoor football and other youth activities.

I had asked where the scaffold was to get to the lights. He had pulled out a folding trestle table and put a big step ladder on top. I had been left there all day on my own, and the only way I could reach the lights was by standing on the very top step. Supporting the weight of the heavy lights as I took them down for repair, I had wobbled dangerously and wondered what would have happened if I fell. I finished the job, but it had left big doubts in my mind.

We were living close to the breadline. We would still have to pay rent, buy food and put fuel in the car and now we had no wage coming in. I was under immense pressure to find a solution. When things were a bit quiet, my boss had sometimes subcontracted me out to another business. Surprisingly, there was much less pressure there and it hadn't been a problem to take tea breaks when I needed them.

The boss of this business told me about another contractor that had landed a big job wiring up a newly built hospital in South Auckland. I gave him a ring and he asked me to come to see him on site the next day. There were no interviews, certificates or references. This was the New Zealand way and I liked it. He showed me around the site and asked me when I could start. I started the following Monday. Initially, I only planned to work there until my original employer was ready to start back. However, the rate of pay he was offering seemed very generous compared with that of my previous employer.

"Just send me an invoice at the end of the month," he said.

Again, I did some maths in my head. It was close to the end of the month and Christmas was upon us. It would be the end of January before I could invoice him and I knew that most companies took time to pay their invoices. I went to see him, cap in hand, and explained my situation. He kindly gave me a couple of weeks' pay upfront, even though I had only just started.

I knew it wouldn't be enough to tide us over, but I couldn't ask for more. I figured I would just go to the bank and ask for an overdraft or get some sort of short-term bank loan. I had always had a good credit score and had never been refused any kind of financial assistance from banks in the UK.

But when I went to see him, the bank manager shook his head.

"No, I'm sorry, but you just haven't been in the country long enough. We don't know enough about you," he said.

My heart sank. I offered my car as collateral, but as it was old and worth very little, he declined.

"What about a credit card, then?" I asked. I discovered there was no chance of a flexible friend either.

I have always been self-sufficient and have never liked relying on others for anything. It's not in my nature to ask for help, as I had always managed somehow. But sometimes we are humbled by our circumstances. This was an occasion when I didn't have any options other than to phone someone back home and ask for help.

I asked one of my brothers to bail me out. I still had a UK bank account, so it was relatively easy for him to transfer funds so that I could access them in New Zealand. He put enough money in to keep us going and totally saved the day. This was a huge relief, and we could finally breathe again.

We were used to being a little bit extravagant at Christmas. The boys would usually get lots of presents; not only from us, but from all their relatives as well. They never got the latest hi-tech gadgets or any designer gear, but we always made sure they weren't disappointed. Janey had a knack of spotting things they would like throughout the year and stashing them away, but I knew we wouldn't be able to give them the same level of excellence in our new environment.

I bought a couple of used BMX bikes, and Mum, Dad and some of our other family members put money into our bank account so we could also buy the boys presents from them.

Christmas came and we all opened our presents. Phil and Paul were really good and appeared enthusiastic about the gifts they received. Then they rode their bikes up and down the street. Christmas dinner with all the trimmings didn't seem right somehow, as it was really hot outside, so we ate it with little enthusiasm. Afterwards, we went to the beach for a swim. Life was tough, but a swim in the sea costs nothing. Then our friends from church called us up and invited us over. We instantly had access to a swimming pool, hot tub, great food and great company. Perhaps we would get used to life in New Zealand after all!

The work at the hospital site was good. As I was basically self-employed, I could work the hours that suited me. Sometimes I worked extra hours as there were deadlines to meet. Every Friday afternoon the boss would come around with pizza and a chilly bin (cool box) filled with cold beer.

I made the decision to remain in this job and sent my previous employer a letter explaining my actions. I felt some obligation to him, as without his job offer I would not have got the visa. However, I knew that it wasn't working out.

Travel to site was a long haul from out east, and I wondered whether we should consider moving to the North Shore. My friend Mark, who lived on the North Shore, told me: "There are two kinds of people who live in Auckland: those who live on the Shore, and those who want to."

It was obviously a nicer area. It had crystal-clear waters and lots of sandy beaches. There were bustling town centres with coffee shops and lots going on.

I saw an apartment advertised in the newspaper for a first-floor flat with a balcony and two bedrooms. Best of all, it was right on the beach. I spoke to the owner, but he said he doubted that it would be big enough for a family like ours. I explained that we were from the UK and used to living in a small terraced house, so he agreed to show us round. It actually had a bigger floor area than our little house in Nantwich had.

I shook hands with the owner and said we would take it. Our friends from church had a courier business and helped us move with their van. We stood on our balcony looking out over the beach and shook our heads in disbelief. Things were definitely looking up.

It was still the summer holidays and the boys spent their days on the beach. Janey could keep an eye on them from the balcony as it was so close. Phil's birthday came along and we bought him a bodyboard so he could have fun riding the waves, but Paul was upset that he didn't have one. It wasn't his birthday, but Phil said he didn't mind his brother getting one as well.

Sometimes I would come home from work to find they had built some huge sand structure on the beach or dug a deep hole. There were days when I would just park the car, take my shirt off and run straight into the sea in my shorts.

We saw a lot more of our North Shore friends, Mark and Nikki, at this time. They didn't live far away, and we were often invited over for barbecues and Sunday lunches. We always felt at home with them. They didn't have children at the time, so they enjoyed teasing ours instead. One summer evening we had a big water fight. It started with someone firing a water pistol and quickly escalated to hosepipes and buckets. We all got soaked, but it was a really good laugh.

I was often asked to preach at the church back in the city suburbs. I would sometimes still be feverishly working away trying to get my sermon notes finished on the Sunday morning. Thankfully, the folks at church were very relaxed and liked the message short and sweet; challenging, but with plenty of humour.

We had been in the country for close to a year by this point and I couldn't remember the last time someone had called me "Mr Ricketts". Even the bank manager called me "James", and I liked it that way. New Zealanders, it would seem, were not known for being formal.

We slowly adjusted to New Zealand life, and particularly to life in Auckland. It was a big city, spread out over a huge area. Each day as I drove home from work over the harbour bridge there was a section of road where Rangitoto Island could be clearly seen across the harbour. Every time I saw it I was reminded of the view of Holyhead mountain that could be seen across the inland sea. It looked so familiar.

Sometimes I felt a little homesick; not for the place itself, but for our family and friends. Keeping in touch was a little easier once we bought a fax machine. Every week we would receive long messages via Simon, who also had one. Sometimes I would hear a funny story about Simon from another family member over the phone and would draw a funny cartoon and fax it to him. He would wonder how news could travel so fast! Computers, internet and emails were still out of our reach.

There was a large retail park nearby, and one afternoon we decided to have a walk around the many shops. Janey liked craft and clothes shops, while I preferred electrical shops. There was a really big computer store and I was drawn to the vast array of computers and laptops on offer, but the prices seemed high.

A salesman assured me that with their easy payments I could have a tailor-made machine that would suit my needs. I sat down and asked him to explain it all to me. He started writing out the credit agreement and then went away to get something. Out of the blue, I felt uneasy. I was suddenly in turmoil. Something didn't feel right at all. I leant over his side of the desk, grabbed the paperwork, ripped it up and walked out of the shop. As soon as I walked outside my peace returned.

Over the years, I have got used to the way God sometimes speaks to us. When we are in God's will, we experience peace. When we're walking the right path, his peace guides us. If we step outside His will, things suddenly

All Things Worked Together for Good

get uncomfortable. The peace disappears. Then we step back into His will and the peace returns. That's what had happened in the computer store. I guess God knew that I had been tempted by the finance deal to get a flashy computer. But did I need it? No. Getting into debt clearly wasn't what God wanted for me.

The months passed by and I had been working hard at the hospital. Getting paid was always a hassle, but I would eventually receive my cheque. Our living standards gradually improved and we added a few bits of furniture, so our apartment almost started to look normal. I had bought a car not long after arriving in the country. I hadn't seen a single rusty car in the area and assumed it was the warmer climate and lack of salt on the roads that kept the cars rust-free. In actual fact, each car had to be inspected every six months. If there was any visible rust it could fail. As a result, people often painted over the rust as soon as it became visible.

My car had looked pristine when I bought it from a car fair. It was a Honda Accord without a mark on it, and it drove really nicely. The car had a sunroof, which would have been useful in the UK as we all like to make the most of the sunshine! In New Zealand the sun shone through and I would get sunburn on my head and legs as I wore shorts most of the time.

I started to notice something strange about the car. If it had been raining for a while and I applied the brakes, at a road junction for example, a river of rusty water would pour out of the roof lining around the sunroof and down my back. I investigated one day and found that the area around the sunroof was riddled with rust, which was making the sunroof leak into the car whenever it rained. Rust was also beginning to bubble through elsewhere.

Thankfully, DIY car repairs were nothing new to me, so I sealed the rusty sunroof and patched the rusty bodywork up as best as I could to keep it roadworthy.

The phone rang one day and I picked it up. It was someone from Elim's head office.

"Do you want a church?" he asked. He told me it was in a farming community about a hundred and fifty kilometres south of North Shore. "Well?" he probed.

It seemed he wanted an answer right away. I asked, "Could I think about it? Could I pray about it?"

I had almost forgotten why we were there; why we had come to New Zealand in the first place. Our vision was finally becoming a reality. I told him we would take a look at it, and when I told Janey the news she was excited. We had become quite comfortable living by the beach, and I felt a bit guilty about the thought of making the family move again, but the reaction was mainly positive.

The next weekend we drove down the main highway and then across the country, arriving in plenty of time for the morning service. We had told the boys to keep quiet about why we were there. We were used to looking smart on Sundays, so we were in our best clothes. I had opted for a suit and tie.

We had planned to remain incognito, sitting quietly at the back and observing, but we were rumbled straight away by the church elder. There was a shared lunch after the meeting, so we went along and chatted to some of the locals. Afterwards we were invited to the outgoing pastor's house and he told us a bit about the church.

The church wasn't big, but it had a good solid core of dedicated believers. A full-time position would have been nice, but that wasn't an option. We had a good look around the town, checking out local property prices and rental possibilities while we were there.

When we returned home, we prayed and mulled it over. Was this what God wanted for us? After a few days it started to feel like it was the right move. I excitedly phoned home and told Dad about it. As he had many years' experience in ministry, he was a source of great wisdom to me and offered us lots of helpful advice.

A few weeks later, we were off again. This time we employed a removals company to move us and the church covered some of the costs. We said goodbye to our little apartment and headed south with an air of excitement.

Away from the big city, property rental was a lot cheaper. We arrived at our rented bungalow, which had four bedrooms, a huge lounge, a big garden, and a large double garage with a workshop and summerhouse. I calculated that the garage area alone was about the same size as our little apartment on the beach. Best of all, there was a swimming pool around the back. Amazingly the rent was considerably less; in fact, it was about half the amount we had been paying for the apartment.

One night, we heard a sound like a World War Two air raid siren. It startled me and I jumped out of bed. What did it mean? I thought it might be a civil defence emergency of some sort; an earthquake, a tsunami or a volcanic eruption, perhaps. Living where we were, these were all real possibilities.

I turned on the TV to see if there were any announcements, and then looked up and down the road. No one else seemed to be up. Eventually, I went back to bed. I asked someone the next day what the siren had been about. Apparently, that was how they summoned the fire service when they were needed. Surely pagers would have been better! It seemed that out there in the sticks the old ways were still heavily relied upon.

As there was no full wage available through the church, I needed to find suitable employment. We weren't too far away from a city, and I managed to get a job as a maintenance electrician at a factory that made agricultural and security products. It was about a half-hour drive from our new home. The work was fairly easy, as I had held similar positions before. It basically involved servicing and repairing machines and keeping production going, although sometimes there would be a project or a new installation. I joined a team of four technicians and we soon became good friends.

Chapter Eleven

The Reverend James

We soon settled into the life of the church and got to know our new congregation well. Someone once told me that when you join a church as the new pastor, twenty percent will love you, twenty percent will hate you and the remaining sixty percent will be indifferent. I think that's a pretty accurate representation.

Paul was enrolled at the primary school in the town. The staff made sure he was properly looked after, and it had a special needs unit, so they were able to give him one-to-one attention. He made really good progress right from the start. In fact, he developed so well that the next summer, when his year group was scheduled to go away on a camping trip he expressed an interest in going. We weren't sure how he would get on, but he went and had a really good time.

Strangely, we noticed that Paul always brought home the drink we sent him to school with. He never seemed to drink it. He would eat his lunch, but for some reason he never drank the drink. We needed to find out why. It turned out he was terrified of the noise the urinals in the boys' toilets made when they flushed. As a young boy, he had often held his hands over his ears at the supermarket as he was scared of the noise that came from fridges or fans.

Paul knew that if he consumed his drink it would only be a matter of time before he needed to go to the dreaded boys' toilets, so he avoided doing so. But as we were living in a fairly hot climate, drinking plenty of fluids was important.

We had a word with his teacher and Paul was given a key to a special toilet, which was normally reserved for the disabled. After a while the teacher decided to help Paul get over this problem. She made a tape recording of the toilets flushing and played it to Paul, explaining why it made the noise. From that moment on he was happy to use the boys' toilets.

Phil went to the intermediate school, which comprised the first two years of secondary school and then college. He settled in really well and seemed to excel in the area of IT. We got him a second-hand PC for his birthday and he would spend hours playing around on it. Before long, he was quite an expert. Whenever we had problems with our computer we would ask Phil to take a look. A roll of the eyes, a shake of the head and a few keystrokes later, the problems would usually disappear.

All Things Worked Together for Good

Our house was really nice and we often hosted church events, such as parties and barbecues. At these times our thoughts would return to the kind of barbecues we used to have back home, with the burnt sausages and charred burgers. Here we had inch-thick steaks, chicken and sausages with cheese inside.

The video camera would come out and we would make videos of ourselves cooking the steaks and having fun. Every so often we would send a video back home. Dad also made videos of the family and sent them back to us.

We bought the boys a big trampoline, as these seemed to be a must-have item in our area. Most of the houses seemed to have one in the garden. Many hours were spent bouncing up and down on it with their friends.

The big circular swimming pool was another big draw. A lot of other children attended our church social gatherings and knew to bring their swimming gear. Phil would shout "Whirlpool!" and everyone in the pool would try to run in a circular pattern, which would make a great big whirlpool in the middle of the pool. In the hot weather I would throw in a deckchair and sit with just my head above the water.

I was asked to conduct a wedding one Saturday. This was something I had never done, and I was a bit nervous about the prospect. The groom was the son of one of our church members. Introductions were made at the family home and plans for the big day were discussed. The bride was Taiwanese and her name was difficult to pronounce. I decided at the time that I had better not get her name wrong and made sure I had it correct in my mind. The groom was called Trevor, so there were no problems there!

I began studying the manual issued to all ministers in training. Within this book there was a sample wedding service with fictitious names. The groom in the manual was called Steven. I began reading it over and over, memorising key parts of the ceremony. I didn't want to leave anything to chance.

The big day arrived. I nervously stood at the front waiting for the bride to arrive and join the groom in front of me. I began the ceremony and read out the vows. For some reason, I kept referring to the groom as Steven, probably because I had memorised the sample service in the manual!

Each time, the groom would repeat, 'Steven?' with a puzzled look on his face and I would say, 'Sorry, Trevor.' This happened several times and was a bit embarrassing to say the least! Once the service was over, the photographs were taken indoors due to the heavy rain.

Taiwanese culture involves candles. Lots of candles. Lit candles were placed around the hall and two candles were used together to light a third, symbolising the union between the two families.

At one point, the bride was asked to take a couple of steps back to facilitate a better photograph. Unfortunately, the headdress got a little too close to the flame of a candle and ignited. The groom quickly came to the rescue and managed to pat out the flames with his hands. Thankfully there were no injuries, but the bride was walking around with smoke rising from the top of her head!

I could contain my laughter no more and let it out, exclaiming "Did anyone get that on video? We could get five hundred dollars for this on *TV Bloopers*!"

All Things Worked Together for Good

There were no smiles or laughter in response. It seemed that no one else shared my sense of humour or thought the episode was in any way funny. I quietly headed home.

There was a big mountain nearby, which was about the same height as Snowdon. A gravel track weaved its way up the mountain, and about halfway up there was a small car park. To get to the summit you had to climb over the gate and walk up the track. There was a transmitter station at the top, and thick vegetation and native bush covered the mountain, even near the top. This was so different from the mountains I was used to, where only grass and heather would survive because of the cold. I often came and walked up the mountain, sometimes alone, as it was a good place to contemplate and talk to God.

I had been quite into mountain biking back in the day and some colleagues and I had been talking about it at the factory. They had been planning a trip up this particular mountain that weekend.

I said: "I'd love to come, but sadly I don't have a bike anymore."

To be honest, I was trying to get out of it. Many years had passed since I had cycled, and my fitness levels certainly weren't what they had been.

"Don't you worry about that. There's a spare bike," my colleague piped up.

So that was that. Saturday morning came, and I met with the guys at the foot of the mountain. I was expecting to drive up to the car park and then continue from there. They had other ideas and wanted to set off from the bottom of the mountain. After a short stretch of cycling I was having trouble keeping up with the rest of the group. When we reached the halfway point, I felt I could go no further.

"I can't go on," I said pathetically. "You carry on and I'll meet you all back here on the way down."

The group set off up to complete their ascent. I lay down on the grass and had a bottle of water and a muesli bar. After a while, I felt much better.

I could hear a truck coming up the track in the distance. I thought to myself 'I wonder, if the truck would stop and offer me a lift if I look like I'm really tired and push my bike.'

It was a long shot, but I lifted the bike over the gate and carried on walking upwards, pushing the bike and exaggerating my tired appearance, hoping the driver would feel sorry for me and offer me a lift. I heard him open the gate and slam his cab door shut before continuing up the mountain in my direction.

"Wanna lift, mate?" asked the driver.

I thanked him, put the bike in the back and relaxed with a smile on my face.

Twenty minutes or so later, I spotted the rest of the group up ahead. By this time they were all pushing their bikes and were red-faced, puffing and panting as they went. I ducked down so they couldn't see me in the cab. I soon reached the summit and lay down on the grass, admiring the lovely view of the sea in the distance. I ate the rest of my lunch while I waited for them.

About an hour later they arrived, still pushing their bikes.

"What took you so long?" I said with a smug grin.

The look on their faces was priceless! It was soon time for the descent, and I had been looking forward to it. We raced down the mountain track, letting gravity do its thing. We talked about that day many times at the factory.

I was initially disappointed that I hadn't been offered a full-time church position. However, the work at the factory was fairly laidback and fitted in well with my work, life, ministry and family balance. The team I was part of were a friendly bunch and we laughed and joked and poked fun at each other. There was a chaplain who wandered around the factory every week. She was a really nice lady. There were limits to what she could do and say, but she was a great listener. Many people in the factory took the time to talk with her; sometimes about personal problems and difficulties, and other times just for a general chat.

I was always happy to chat if she had time. After a while, she told me that one of my factory colleagues had been very wary of me before I came. They had all known from the start that I was also a church minister. He had told the chaplain, "Well, he'd better not start preaching at me," and explained what he would do if I did. There had been a clear implication of violence!

His defences had been up, ready for me, as soon as I started. After a short while she had asked him what he thought of me. "He's like no minister I've ever known," he told her.

I smiled when I heard this, as I always try to be myself. Prior to this, I would have tried hard to make people like me in a new situation, and this often had the opposite effect. I guess he hadn't expected me to be a 'normal' person and I felt honoured that he had said that about me.

James Ricketts

I never kept quiet about my faith, but there is a time and a place to talk about it. I was getting paid to do a job, so it wouldn't have been right for me to spend all day evangelising. I was always on time, did my work as best I could and tried to be nice to people. Then I waited until I was asked a question about faith. You often have to earn the right to tell people about the way God has affected your life.

I also bought everyone in the workshop a Bible. It made me smile when I came into the workshop each morning and saw these Bibles on the shelves over a line of benches, along with a load of machine manuals and tools.

Back at the church, Janey had decided to lead the worship team. There was a pianist, a drummer, a guitarist, several singers and a bass player. Prior to this, she would have shrunk back from such a challenge. When we first met, she had been quiet and a bit self-conscious. She would never have dreamed of doing anything that involved any kind of leadership. But something had happened at Bible College. Janey and some of the other women had often gone to renewal meetings at another church about an hour away. People there would pray for them after the service and many lives were changed as a result.

One day around this time Janey had announced that she wanted to address all the women at the college. However, you couldn't just decide to have a meeting at college. Permission from the principal was required.

Permission had been granted, and she had set about making up personalised invitations for all the ladies. On the day of the meeting, the college chapel was full. Janey had preached with a real passion and people had gone away encouraged and inspired. I wasn't allowed in to hear her for

All Things Worked Together for Good

myself as it was ladies only, but I was so proud of her. God had done such an amazing thing in her life.

As with any church position, change is necessary. We were completely new to leading a church and still relatively new to the country. Sometimes we got it wrong and sometimes there were cultural differences. Sometimes we would get the wrong end of the stick or fail to understand local customs. I have never liked church politics, and as a leader I had a dilemma on my hands. Whatever I did, some people would be pleased but others would be upset. Trying to please everybody was a lose-lose situation. I realised a lot of energy and enthusiasm would be wasted with this approach.

Quite a few members of the congregation were Maori, and one of the Maori men became a good friend of mine. It was good to talk to him about the research I had done while writing my thesis. He was a chief and told me about the way he and his people lived. One day, he took me to the Marae. Each tribe has its own cultural centre, and this was theirs.

I had read up about the protocol of what you should and shouldn't do in these places. He took me into the meeting hall, which was resplendent with wooden arches, polished wooden floors and ornate carvings. I started taking my shoes off to protect the floors and show my respect.

He looked startled. "What are you doing?" he asked.

"Well, I thought..." I began, feeling a bit nervous.

"You don't have to bother with that. You're with the chief now," he replied.

I felt honoured and blessed to have been brought to a place like this, and for not having been required to take my shoes off.

The church experienced some growth quite early on. Often when a new minister is appointed there is transfer growth from other churches. Some may not be very committed to a particular church and choose to float from place to place. There were also new families who had recently moved into the area for work. I had hoped that we would see considerable growth, and that I would be able to work full time at the church. However, it was a small agricultural community and a lot of our members were quite poor. As it happened, I quite enjoyed the factory job, so it wasn't a problem.

Every year, the church denomination we were part of had its annual conference. The previous year (1998) it had been in Wellington, a long drive south in our tatty Honda with Janey and the boys. As the conference was largely about church business, it wasn't really a good place for children.

This year (1999), the conference was to be in Christchurch, on the South Island. Flights had been booked for Janey and me. We were to fly from Hamilton into Wellington, then on to Christchurch. The boys would stay with a couple from the church who had a farm out in the country.

We arrived at the airport and I was surprised to find that I would be parking my car in a grassy field. Our bags were checked in and I looked out the window to see where our plane was. We had only flown a couple of times by this point and always on large aircraft like 747s. I asked one of the staff which was our aircraft and showed her my ticket. She pointed over to another grassy area and said, "That's your plane over there." It was very small and had propellers. I wasn't impressed, and neither was Janey!

Janey kept her eyes closed during take-off, but I was still fascinated by flying and looked out of the window. I pointed out some landmarks that came into view as we banked steeply. She shook her head with her eyes still tightly shut. There were about ten people on board, plus a pilot and one flight attendant. It was very noisy, and the little plane seemed to shake about a lot. I must admit I was nervous, but I couldn't show it, of course, as I felt men should be brave!

Wellington was notorious for being a windy place and the day we arrived was no exception. The plane was bouncing around a lot and there was a lot of turbulence. My hands were gripping the back of the seat in front of me tightly and my knuckles had turned white. The plane would suddenly drop at intervals and veer to the left and right.

I was certain that we were going to die that day! I started praying and searched my mind, making sure I didn't have any grudges against anyone and had no outstanding need to forgive anyone who had wronged me. Forgiveness is a key element in the Christian life. If we don't forgive, the Bible teaches that we are not forgiven, so I made sure no one was missed out. I also thought about the boys. Who would look after them if we didn't make it?

As we made our final approach, the crosswind was so bad that we were approaching the runway at a bit of an angle. I could see right up the runway out of my side window. 'Surely that's not right,' I thought. I closed my eyes and waited for the impact. I was ready to die and so was Janey.

But there was no impact. A screech of tyres signalled that we were back on solid ground and everyone cheered. As it was such a small aircraft, exiting the plane was just a matter of climbing down a short ladder onto the concrete. As soon as I was off the plane I knelt down and kissed the concrete, much to the amusement of the other passengers and crew.

We were welcomed by the conference organisers and shown around the city, even taking in a tram ride. I was surprised to see a lot of slate roofs, red-brick buildings and traditional red telephone boxes like the ones we see in rural Britain. It reminded me of back home. Another thing that reminded me of home was the weather! We were much closer to Antarctica and there was a cold blast coming from the Southern Alps. I hadn't felt that chilly in quite a while.

The conference was great, and we were encouraged to attend the sessions of various inspirational speakers. The accommodation was also nice. There were other pastors and wives we knew at the conference and it was a good opportunity to catch up with people we didn't see very often.

I had already been in ministry in New Zealand for a couple of years, but this conference was to have even greater significance for us, as I was to be ordained. That's right! I officially became Reverend James. Funnily enough, I had been nicknamed this by work colleagues in the past as they knew I was a Christian and could be a bit overzealous at times!

All Things Worked Together for Good

There was an English family at the church. Dave worked for the water authority, looking after a water treatment plant out in the country. Possums were a big problem in New Zealand, as they would strip the bark from native trees and spread disease among cattle. As a result, poison was often used to control their numbers. Because of the proximity to the town reservoir, it wasn't permitted to use poison in that area, so there was only one other way to control them: with a gun. And not an air gun, either; a proper rifle.

One evening, there was a knock at the door and it was Dave.

"Fancy coming out to shoot possums?" he asked.

How could I refuse such an offer? We set off for the forest with rifles and a backpack containing a battery with a handheld spotlight. One of us would shine the light up into the trees and, on seeing a pair of eyes looking back into the light, the other would shoot. There would be a loud noise as the animal came crashing down through the branches and landed on the forest floor. We had to be careful which direction we shot in as there were some houses in certain areas near the forest. I felt a bit mean shooting them to start off with, but they were a national pest and I was doing the country a good service. At least, that's what I was told.

Mark and Nikki visited often, and we went to stay in Auckland with them whenever we had a chance. Mark was a keen surfer. I was envious, as it looked like great fun. I was a good swimmer and could catch a wave on a body board, so it looked like something I would enjoy.

I got hold of a second-hand board and fitted roof bars to the car. Week after week I would go to one of the nearby beaches. Every time I caught a wave I would fall off, and Mark thought I had bought the wrong kind of board. Someone at work heard about my struggles and offered me a big Mini Mal board, thinking it would be better for me. It wasn't in tip-top condition and needed repairs, but he didn't want much for it. I spent the next day working on it with some fibreglass, and then it was ready.

My new board was more than eight feet long and had a single fin at the back. The next weekend I took it out to a beach on the east coast where there was always waves. I parked the car and headed for the beach with my board under my arm.

There was only a small wave coming in, at perhaps two or three feet high. The biggest challenge was getting out behind the waves. This time, I managed to get out quite quickly. I saw a wave and started paddling the way Mark had taught me. Then, in one fluid movement, I made the move to get up on my feet. It worked! I was doing it! I was surfing properly; standing up on a board. It almost felt like walking on water! I was whooping and shouting with delight. What a buzz!

Chapter Twelve

"I Want What You Want"

Later that year, Simon came to visit. He was still at Bible college but had a couple of weeks off. I decided to take him on a road trip up north and Phil came with us. It would be quite an experience for him.

I took a few days off work, Phil had a few days off school, and we headed up north. I showed Simon some of the sights, including the beautiful beaches and forests. We stayed at a motor camp that Janey and I had stayed at a few years previously when we had visited the country for a month.

There was a big beach that stretched for miles, and the locals would drive their cars onto it. After having some fun doing handbrake turns on the beach, I allowed Phil to have a go at driving the car. He was twelve years old and behind the wheel of a car! I sat behind him on the driver's seat to make sure he didn't go too fast. At first he was quite careful, but as his confidence grew he started going faster. There was always a danger of getting stuck or the tide coming in and washing over the cars on beaches like this, so care was needed.

Simon came to church with us on the Sunday and one of our older members approached us. He was a godly man but was known to be a little bit nosey and was always asking newcomers lots of questions. I decided to have a bit of fun with him.

I introduced Simon and said: "This is my brother Simon. I'm afraid he doesn't speak English. He was born in Wales and the rest of the family had to learn Welsh so we could understand him when he started talking."

He started talking to Simon loudly and making exaggerated head movements in a bid to make himself understood.

"Welcome, welcome, welcome," he said loudly and animatedly.

I translated this for Simon: "Croeso, croeso, croeso," I said.

My Welsh is limited and I'm not really fluent, but Simon replied with a few sentences I understood and I relayed them back to the man in English. We continued like for a few minutes.

Eventually, we could keep it up no longer and burst out laughing. This poor church member was not impressed.

"There are two jokers in every pack!" he barked and stormed off furiously.

I liked a joke, but perhaps we had gone too far this time.

All Things Worked Together for Good

By the time Phil was in college (for children aged thirteen to eighteen), Paul had started intermediate school (for children aged ten to thirteen). Phil fitted in well and was making good progress, but Paul really struggled at his new school. There was no one-to-one teacher, no special needs class and no special consideration of his difficulties. Paul was expected to be like every other child in the school and he struggled to keep up with the work. He was really stressed by the situation and even spoke of taking his own life. This was heart-breaking for us and we knew something had to be done. Something drastic.

We discovered that it was possible to take him out of school and teach him ourselves as long as we could demonstrate that we had the resources and capability to give him an education. We would even get a grant every six months towards his books and resources. It was no picnic, but after a while we felt we were ready to take the step.

Although Paul was about twelve by this time, he still couldn't read. "Reading is impossible," he would say. We would point at words and he would just reel off others that started with the same first letter.

After about a week of home schooling, I came home from work one day and was amazed. Paul was reading *The New Zealand Herald*, a broadsheet newspaper. He had always had a fascination with flight and there was an article in the paper about *the Hindenburg* disaster. He was able to read it perfectly! It turned out that it was all about confidence. Once he gained this confidence he was able to read books and find information for himself. Janey taught him a range of subjects, while I taught him maths, science and practical tasks.

James Ricketts

We noticed that he had a special interest in space and the planets. In the evenings, he would spend hours outside and even created a map of the universe. He had binoculars, but a telescope would have been even better, so eventually we got him one. Paul liked to categorise data, make charts and reel off facts and figures. He could tell you everything about any planet: size, distance from the sun, temperature, mass, density and gravitational force.

When he spoke, he used long, scientific words. Sometimes he would start his sentences by saying, "My calculations seem to suggest..."

He also liked collections of things. It started with toy hedgehogs, and then he developed an interest in birds of prey, followed by seashells. As well as collecting on the sea shores, he would buy tropical specimens from street markets with his pocket money. He soon had a collection of more than eight hundred shells, housed in glass cases and drawers. He knew most of the Latin names as well as the scientific names, and knew everything about where they could be found, their habitat and so forth. We wondered whether Paul was exhibiting behaviour that might have placed him on the autism spectrum, but we didn't really know where to turn for advice.

After about three years we found that we were struggling to run the church, earn a living and have enough family time. We were drawn to the idea of moving back to Auckland. I felt guilty about having to uproot Phil from his college yet again, but as it was the summer holidays, at least he would be starting a fresh term. We resigned from the church but remained on good terms with everyone.

All Things Worked Together for Good

I began making enquiries about work opportunities in Auckland. I had sent my CV to some friends in the hope that they might know of a suitable position. Nikki had a job with a telecommunications company and was in the middle of a meeting with someone from a company they used to work on their network and for their telephone exchanges. My CV happened to be open on her computer screen and the man asked about it, as they were looking for technicians. I was already in the city visiting another potential employer when my phone rang. He explained who he was and asked if I could meet him that day!

He told me where their main offices were, and I managed to find the place. I had a case full of certificates and references, but as usual no one wanted to see them. After a ten-minute chat, he asked me "When can you start?"

I was really pleased. I agreed to start in a couple of weeks' time and began making the arrangements. We found a small house to rent and I gave notice at the factory.

We moved our things to the new place on the North Shore, fairly close to the apartment we had rented a few years earlier. The first time I opened the sliding door that led out to the garden, a large cockroach dropped to the floor and scuttled off. I hoped it had come from the outside.

Unfortunately, it hadn't, and over the next few weeks we found them everywhere. I would wake up in the morning and there would be one on the wall looking at me. We realised the place was infested. I contacted the letting agent. I said that we wanted out, and that we expected to get our letting fee back. We found a better place around the corner and moved again. This one was about the same size but had no cockroaches, so we were able to settle.

James Ricketts

The job was interesting and varied. During my time at the factory I had learned to look after the network and phone systems. I was also experienced in data cabling. I was doing that kind of work all the time in this job for banks, telecommunication companies and large retail customers. I had my own van and would be sent all over the Auckland area. The slow pace of country living was behind me now. I was an Aucklander, living a fast-paced life.

We did miss church life, however. As a member of a small church you know everyone's name, at the very least, and hopefully they also know yours, especially if you're the pastor! We started going along to one of the bigger city churches. We really wanted to get involved, but it seemed like we were hitting a brick wall each time. The thought crossed my mind that perhaps we should have stayed where we were.

I had envisaged becoming part of the music team or something like that and had hoped that I could perhaps become an assistant pastor at a large church. Sadly, every door seemed to be closed. Every week we would go along and try to get to know people, but it was difficult with so many in the congregation.

At least we were close to our friends again, and Mark and I often went surfing together. I loved my new board and it seemed perfect for me. I could catch even small waves on it with no problem. Sometimes, when I was feeling brave, I would try to catch really big waves.

Mount Maunganui is a popular surfing spot, and we spent a day there on one occasion. A big wave came from behind me and carried me up onto the crest. It felt like I was on top of a house looking down at the ground. It was really

All Things Worked Together for Good

big. There was a split-second decision to make: back off and let the wave go, or shift my body weight forward and take off down the face of the giant wave.

I decided to take it on. I shot down the face of the wave and tried t stand. The nose of the board dug into the wave and I came off. The wave broke and came crashing down on top of me. There was a lot of water!

I was thrashing about, not even knowing which way was up, and all the time I was tethered to the board, which was being propelled towards the shore as the wave broke. I remember thinking that I hadn't breathed in quite a while and the thought crossed my mind that I might drown. Somehow, I managed to get to the surface, grabbed my board for buoyancy and took a deep breath.

Another day when the conditions were better I got it right and the wave carried me right into the shore. I just stepped off it, picked up the board and walked up the beach.

Sometimes my work took me to interesting places. There was a Sky tower in the city, which was useful to the telecommunications companies because of its height. I was asked to do some work in the communications room on level forty-nine. It offered a three-hundred-and-sixty-degree view of the city, with floor to ceiling windows. What a view, and all from two hundred metres up in the air!

My work involved making connections in a panel close to a very large dish, which emitted microwave radiation for mobile phone signals. There were warning signs all over it telling workers not to come within two metres of it. Here I was standing right up against it. I asked my account manager if it was safe.

James Ricketts

He replied: "What I do is put a meat pie in my pocket. If it starts getting hot, I know I'm too close."

I hoped he was joking.

By this time, I was on a call-out rota. I would often get called out to places like this in the evenings and even in the middle of the night. If the call came in at a reasonable time, I would sometimes take one of the boys with me. Paul was particularly interested in the high-rise buildings. Usually, it was a simple job of resetting a switch or something like that, but it was an experience for the boys nonetheless.

Simon came to visit us again, and this time he brought his wife, Anita. As I had a big van at my disposal, I gave Simon the use of my car so they could spend a few days travelling around and seeing some of the sights. By this point I had a much better, more modern car with air conditioning, so it was more comfortable to cruise around in. They spent three weeks with us before heading back to Wales.

Over the next few months we began to think about the possibility of moving back to Wales. After nearly five years in New Zealand we were missing the place. It was so expensive for the four of us to travel that the idea of a holiday was out of the question. Although I was in a good job, the earnings still weren't enough to provide a good a standard of living, mainly as accommodation near the city was so expensive. The reality was that we would never be able to afford to buy a home and settle properly unless something incredible happened.

I took some time out and went hiking in the bush near the mountain I used to walk up. It was a time for me to talk to God and ask questions, as well as just enjoying the countryside.

As I was walking, I asked God, "What do you want?"

I wasn't sure what kind of answer to expect, but as clear as anything, I heard God say: "I want what you want, James."

It seemed like a vague kind of answer, but I knew exactly what I wanted. I wanted to be in the only place I could really call home: Wales.

It was a good time to make the move, as Phil was fifteen and in college. Paul was also progressing well with his studies. If we had left it much later, the boys might have been in further education, or have embarked on set career paths, or have been in committed relationships. It wouldn't have been so straightforward in those circumstances. We talked about the idea of returning home and everyone had a say. The general consensus was that we should head back to Wales.

One problem was the education system back home. Phil would be expected to go to the high school in Holyhead, and he was adamant that he wouldn't go. What could we do? We contacted the education authority in North Wales and asked for advice. Because Phil was very good with computers, there was an opportunity for him to do an IT course at a college rather than going back to school.

He had done some work setting up networks for a couple of businesses, and at one point we had received lots of phone calls for Phil as he was the technical support worker. These businesses gave us references that we could forward to the college and he was accepted onto the course. We also wondered about Paul as there was no way we could send him to the high school.

In order to make the move back we needed a fair sum of money, so I needed to cash in an investment. Because we were in another country, this made the process complex and lengthy. Once the finances were in and transferred to my New Zealand bank account, we could start booking flights, getting removals organised and things like that. We decided that we didn't want to end up back home with no furniture as we had when we first arrived in New Zealand.

After a few weeks I received the phone call I had been waiting for. The money had cleared and was on its way to my account. I was at work when the call came in, and I did all I could to contain my excitement. I hadn't yet given notice or any indication that I was planning to leave. I gave a couple of weeks' notice, booked our flights and employed a removals company to pack away our things and put them in a container for shipping. We let the men take away most of the furniture and stayed in the house with the bare essentials. After all, it would only be for a couple of weeks.

I sold my car and a friend lent us theirs as they were out of the country. Then I started tying up all the loose ends. Having finished work the week before we decided to stay with Mark and Nikki for the last week.

We only had one week left in New Zealand! Friends we had made over the years came round to the house for a bit of a send-off. I was excited and apprehensive at the same time. What would I do for work? Where would we live? In the five years we had lived in New Zealand, the only relatives we had seen were Simon and Anita. We were so looking forward to seeing everyone again, and this took the edge off the apprehension.

All Things Worked Together for Good

The day arrived. Our bags were packed and weighed, and our hand luggage was sorted. I would need tools if I was going to get a job, so I packed a briefcase full of essential tools. Mark and Nikki drove us to the airport, and I stopped at the bank on the way. I closed my account and took out the remaining money in cash. A group of people from the church we had pastored had also come to see us off, and there was enough time for us to have a coffee and a chat with our friends.

The boys were excited about the flight, but I wasn't too bothered. It would be a ten-hour flight to Hong Kong, fourteen more to Amsterdam, and then a final hour's flight into Manchester. I quite liked flying, but it could become boring. The take-off was exciting, the food and drinks were nice when they came around, and the landing was always a relief, but all the hours in between were mundane. I could never sleep, as most passengers did on long-haul flights.

Eventually the time came for us to go through security and head for the gate. We said our goodbyes and I gave Phil all the remaining New Zealand change I had so he could buy any magazines and sweets he and his brother wanted. The rest of the money had been changed into sterling ready for our new adventure.

As I sat on the plane, it felt as if something was missing. I was used to having a bunch of keys in my pocket. There I sat with no house keys, car keys or work keys. All I had was my empty keyring with the sawn-in-half fifty pence piece on it. It had worked. Every time I had looked at it, I had remembered Dad and his slightly eccentric ways. I was so looking forward to seeing him, my mum and my brothers, as well as all the extended family.

James Ricketts

We were met at Manchester by Dad and Pete, a friend of ours from college days. For the previous five years or so he had been the pastor of my home church in Holyhead. Dad looked a bit older and greyer, but he seemed well. I gave him a big hug, distributed our bags between the two cars and then we were on our way. It felt strange to be back in the UK again.

We headed down the motorway, which it seemed really fast compared to New Zealand. I had been booked for speeding several times during our time abroad before finally getting used to the lower speed limits. We sped along the North Wales coast and were soon back in my hometown.

Chapter Thirteen

Absence Makes the Heart Grow Fonder

David was living locally at this time. Having been in the police force for years, he had lived in various parts of North Wales. He was working in Holyhead by this point and had a nice big house near the beach. He kindly offered to put us up for a few weeks while we settled back into the swing of things.

I had a few hundred pounds in my pocket from the dollars I had changed at the airport and we also had some money in our bank account left over from the investment I had cashed in. I found an old second-hand car that would be suitable for us and started looking for work.

We had hoped the money in the bank would be enough for a deposit on a house, as we had missed owning our own home in New Zealand. The next morning I was wide awake by about four as I still hadn't adjusted to the time difference. The house was quiet, so I got dressed and slipped out of the front door. I walked the familiar paths around coastal areas and across fields; places that had significance; places I had known since I was a young child.

I arrived back at the house as everyone else was getting up and having breakfast. I told David where I had been. He gave me a stern look and explained that it was actually illegal to walk across the fields because of the outbreak of foot-and-mouth disease among the sheep and cattle. I had heard about it on the news but hadn't even considered it while I was out on my long walk.

I didn't know how long I would be out of work, so I did something I have never had to do in my life. I went to the job centre to see about signing on for Jobseekers' Allowance. They were immediately suspicious of me. They thought that I was perhaps over on holiday and would be going back again. I had to show them papers from the removals company before they were assured that I was genuine. There weren't many jobs in my line of business, but we managed to find one on the other side of the island and I put an application in.

My friend from college, Pete, who was pastor of the local church, had informed me that he was leaving as he had been offered the leadership of a new church in Scotland. The question was, was I interested in taking the position? Janey and I had known about this before we came back and already knew what our answer would be. We said yes and the necessary meetings with the church overseers were set up. In the meantime, I found out I had been successful in my job application and hadn't even needed to start signing on.

All Things Worked Together for Good

The job was a good half-hour drive away. It was factory maintenance work again, which was nothing new for me. The pay was poor, and when I included the expense of driving to and from the factory every day it seemed even worse. I would be called out in the middle of the night and have to travel to the factory to repair the machines, and the payment for these call-outs was minimal. I didn't think I would be staying in this job for long. Thankfully, I didn't have to.

The process of applying for the ministry position at my home church was moving along and a meeting was set up with the church session. Many of the deacons had been friends of the family for years. Some had even taught me in Sunday school as a small child. They knew me well enough, but still needed to ask questions.

The church building had been in a state of disrepair for many years. As a result, the roof and windows had recently been replaced. Because of this, I was informed that there was very little money available to pay a pastor's salary. All they could afford was a small weekly amount for expenses such as fuel and phone calls.

Again, this was nothing new to me and I had a feeling this would be the case. As it happened, still unhappy at my job, I saw an advert in the local paper for an electrician at the aluminium smelter in town. It was where I had been an apprentice in the 1980s. The pay was good and it was a secure job, so I applied straight away. Seventeen years had passed since I had left the plant.

I was soon called in for an interview, and three out of the four people interviewing me remembered me from my apprentice days. Lots of questions were asked, including some technical ones and others about my experience since I had left the plant. As I knew the place well and was familiar with the processes, I flew through the interview and was soon offered a position.

By this time we had bought a house and been reunited with all our belongings. It was nice to be among familiar items, such as our sofa and armchairs. The new house was a big three-storey house with lots of space. Unfortunately, it wasn't in the best part of town and had no garden. Still, it was ours, and right then that was all that mattered.

I began my new job and was shown around the area I would be working in. It felt so strange being there again after all those years. The last time I had been there I had been a twenty-year-old apprentice. A lot of water had flowed under the bridge since then, yet there I was again.

I turned up for work wearing my All Blacks rugby shirt. On top of this, I still had a bit of a Kiwi twang when I spoke. Not everyone knew me from my early days and I noticed some people were a bit wary of me. I soon found out why. The smelter was owned by a huge international mining company. The last time I had been there it was run by Americans. At this time it was run by New Zealanders. It was a bit of a coincidence, and I had no idea this was the case. Not everyone liked the new management, and when the new guy had turned up wearing a New Zealand rugby shirt and speaking with a slight accent they had put two and two together and come up with five.

At around the same time, I was invited to accept the position of pastor at my home church. It felt strange and there was much to do. I wondered how I would manage

All Things Worked Together for Good

running a church and working at the plant. The building needed lots of work, as did our house. Good time management would be essential from that point onwards.

Meanwhile, we had already decided before travelling back home from New Zealand that we would continue educating Paul at home. We didn't contact the education authority, but simply carried on as we had been. Phil had been doing his IT course, travelling every day by bus to the college. He had always been smart.

It turned out the course was quite basic, and he wasn't really challenged enough by it. As a result, he started messing about. He would hack into the college system and give himself extra print credits and things like that. The last straw came when he was caught hacking into the lecturers' accounts. A letter explaining the gravity of the situation was sent to us and he was expelled from the course. This was a bit embarrassing as the education authority had bent over backwards to accommodate Phil.

Later that summer, having had time to reflect, Phil told me about a graphic design course that was starting at the same college.

I said: "Don't be surprised if they don't welcome you back with open arms after what you did."

Fortunately, they did welcome him back. He knew what he wanted and was more focused this time round. He really found his niche and knuckled down to hard work. Three years later he ended up with a triple distinction, and even did some part-time instructing at the college. He made us really proud.

Paul was seventeen by this time. We had done extensive research on his behaviour and had come up with a possible diagnosis. To us, he seemed to have the classic symptoms of Asperger syndrome. This is an autism spectrum disorder. I hated the idea of labelling Paul with some sort of 'disorder', but he certainly had a distinctly different way of looking at things.

He was also brutally honest. For example, if I asked him what he thought of a sermon I had preached, he might say, "Actually, I found it quite boring." If we wanted an honest opinion, Paul was the one to ask as feelings were not spared.

He didn't like wrappers or small bits of rubbish, so these had to be hidden or thrown away immediately. Clothing labels were ripped or cut out. Food had to be eaten in a certain order and tea drunk at specific times of the day. Paul was ruled by routine.

We raised our concerns with the GP and Paul was referred to a psychiatrist. I didn't like the idea of him being examined by a 'shrink', but we went along to the assessment with him. The psychiatrist was Australian and casually dressed. We were expecting a man in a white coat and a couch to recline on while Paul was being questioned, but it wasn't like that at all.

Paul was asked questions, and some of the questions were directed towards us. Paul was also asked to complete some exercises. He had never been good with written work, but he persisted. At the end of the assessment, the psychiatrist completely agreed with our opinion about Asperger's and concluded that Paul had it quite severely. This didn't change anything; Paul was still Paul, but at least we had a better understanding of why he behaved the way he did.

All Things Worked Together for Good

I had always tried to encourage the boys to learn a musical instrument, but neither had showed any interest whatsoever. I didn't want to push it or force lessons on them, so I had left it.

One day, Phil announced: "I think I'd like to learn to play the electric guitar."

I wasted no time. My friend Stuart still lived nearby, and we saw a lot of each other. He had always liked my fish tank, while I had lost interest in it. He offered me a swap for an electric guitar together with an amplifier. I did the deal, then bought a couple of teaching videos and a chord book to give Phil.

Phil occupied the attic bedroom and it wasn't long at all before we heard music coming from his room. I thought he was playing a CD at first, but then I realised he was actually playing the guitar. He seemed to have taken to it really quickly.

Mum and Dad were both retired and I would often go up to their house just to sit and chat. Dad was very wise and had years of experience in church matters, so he would give me helpful advice.

They would often walk in the mountains and covered a lot of distance every month. Gone was the old battered Austin Dad had thought so much of when it was new. It had been replaced with a Volvo and a caravan. They would always be off somewhere with the caravan for weeks at a time. Their favourite place was Devil's Bridge near Aberystwyth. Sometimes they would travel down in the caravan at the start of the season and leave it there all summer. This meant they didn't have the hassle of towing the van every time they wanted to go there.

James Ricketts

Dad had washed his socks at one of the campsites and needed to dry them. He had decided it would be a good idea to drape them over one of the engine cooling pipes to dry. He completely forgot about this and off they went in the car. Dad noticed smoke billowing out from under the bonnet, but even with the smoke he couldn't work it out. He was sure the car was about to burst into flames.

He shouted to Mum: "As soon as I pull over, get out and run away from the car!"

They stopped and made a hasty exit from the car. Nothing dramatic happened, so Dad cautiously went back and opened the bonnet, only to find a pair of very burnt socks on the radiator hose.

Phil had recently upgraded our computer and there were plenty of spare parts to make up a complete system. Mum and Dad didn't have a computer, so on Dad's birthday I presented him with a big box with a full computer system inside. He opened it and I helped set it up.

He was interested in computers, but also a little terrified. Mum went to the library, borrowed a book about computers and started learning how to use it. Dad liked the idea of being able to look up people from his past and reconnect with them. He would get Mum to type out emails as he was too scared to use it.

I called in one day as I often did. Mum looked serious. "You'd better sit down," she said.

I feared that bad news was to follow and did as I was told.

"Your father sent an email today!" she continued.

In the past, he had rattled off letters on his old Royal typewriter, but now he could use a word processor, send emails and connect with the outside world.

All Things Worked Together for Good

"Welcome to the twenty-first century," I joked.

James Ricketts

Chapter Fourteen

Life is a Rollercoaster

The church had grown considerably. Lots of young people had started coming, and this could be a bit of a challenge at times. With the help of some of the church members, we had transformed the back room into a youth centre. There was a stage, new toilets, a kitchen, nice laminate flooring and modern lighting.

Janey had painted the walls and ceiling. She had cleverly downloaded images of skateboarders and printed them onto acetate sheets. She had then used the overhead projector to shine the images onto the walls and then painted them. She also painted some of the areas with a sort of surf swirl pattern that seemed to pay homage to the New Zealand koru, or fern. It looked great. We finished it off with the addition of pool and table tennis tables.

The youth centre was a big hit with the young people in the area, and our Sunday night meetings were adapted to suit them. We never had to put signs out or advertise; they would just come. Perhaps it was the music. I know that just about everyone wanted to play the drums afterwards. The band consisted of Janey on the acoustic guitar, Phil, who by this time was an amazing lead guitarist, another electric guitar and myself on bass, with the addition of a really good drummer.

Sometimes we didn't really know what to play during the evening services. Hymns wouldn't cut it with unchurched youth. One week we had a go at playing an old Status Quo song, 'Rockin' all over the World', but changed the words to Christian lyrics about praising God. After the meeting had closed a young lad came up to me, shaking with excitement. His eyes were wide like saucers.

"That was the best Christian song I've ever heard," he stammered.

To give credit where credit is due, I told him who really wrote the song and how we had just added the words. It did make me smile, though.

After the meeting, people young and old would mingle in the new youth centre, sharing a game of pool, and a cup of tea and a biscuit. Anyone who was disruptive during the meetings would be temporarily barred from playing and I would say, "Let's see how your attitude is next week." It

All Things Worked Together for Good

usually worked. They got the message and would sit through an hour-long meeting, listening to the talk and the gospel invitation, knowing that they would be rewarded with free games of pool afterwards!

The church building needed a lick of paint. We went for a bold colour scheme of blue on the walls with all the mouldings and reliefs picked out in gold. Dad had been the last person to paint the ceiling, which was a huge circular floral relief feature made from plaster. This had been in 1971, shortly after he had arranged the purchase of the former Welsh Chapel.

I would only have been six or seven, but I could remember him lying on his back on top of a scaffold, picking out all the details in pastel shades. Three-and-a-half decades later I had to break it to him that we wanted to paint it again. He wasn't bothered and was quite happy with our choice of colour scheme. I was so glad I had got his blessing to paint the ceiling. This time it was Janey on top of the scaffold with a paintbrush. We finished the job off with a matching carpet and chairs.

A few days later I was called on at work to cover someone who was on holiday for a couple of weeks. This would mean following a shift pattern. I wasn't keen on the night shifts, in particular. I just couldn't sleep during the day. If it was quiet, the fitter and I would watch a film on the TV in our mess room. It wasn't really permitted, but most shifts had a portable TV stashed away in a locker for such occasions. We watched a movie, keeping an ear out for the phone or radio in case there was a breakdown somewhere.

James Ricketts

An hour or so into our film we were interrupted by a production team leader, who needed us straight away. We switched off the TV and headed over to the job in the pickup truck with our tools. For some reason I didn't have my personal mobile phone on me, just the work one.

The phone rang and one of the team leaders told me, "Your brother's been trying to get hold of you. Your dad's not well, and you'd better go home."

I told the fitter who was working with me, and he told me to leave straightaway. I wasn't sure what to think. 'Not well' could mean anything, even a cold or the flu. But why ring me at two in the morning? Dad was fit and healthy, and he was only seventy-three. What could possibly be wrong?

I soon found out, although I couldn't get through to my parents on the phone. He had suffered some kind of stroke in the night and had stopped breathing, so Mum had called an ambulance. The paramedics had resuscitated him, and he was on his way to Bangor Hospital.

I called Simon and told him I would pick him up, and we raced to the hospital together. I didn't care about speeding tickets; I needed to know what was going on. David was already there by the time we got there. He had been on duty that night and had gone straight to the house, so he had seen first-hand what was going on.

Dad was unconscious, and we didn't know what was happening to him. All kinds of tests were being done, but all we could do was wait and pray. Having seen programmes like *ER* and *Casualty*, where a heart attack or stroke victim is usually found sitting up with a cup of tea shortly after being resuscitated, I expected him to wake up at any moment.

All Things Worked Together for Good

We sat in the waiting room expecting to receive some news. Mum's sister, Angela, and her husband, Alan, had been visiting from Australia and were staying with my parents. John was the only one who wasn't close, but we called him and he was soon on his way.

Dad was moved from recovery to the intensive care unit, and we were finally allowed to go and see him. He lay there connected to monitors, with drips in his arms and an oxygen mask over his face.

The results of his tests had come through and we were called into a kind of conference room. We were told, in no uncertain terms, that Dad would not regain consciousness. They said he would probably die from pneumonia in a matter of two to three weeks. But they had given him every possible chance of recovery by putting him on oxygen.

I was heartbroken. As we left his bedside, I went back and said, "Dad, I love you." I can't remember ever telling him that before. We sat silently in the waiting room. I had been trying to contain my emotions, to be strong for Mum, but I was broken and could hold it in no longer. Deep down, I knew he had gone.

After about a week they moved him to a private room. We visited every day. Mum had a driving licence but rarely drove. David had a small hatchback and he gave it to mum for her visits.

I would go every day after work. Because of his physical fitness, Dad was strong inside, but years of high blood pressure and high cholesterol had taken their toll. Fatty deposits had come away from the lining of an artery and travelled up to his brain, starving part of it of oxygen. He had been on medication for years, but his high fitness levels had led me to expect that he would live to a ripe old age.

For quite some time we were believing for a miracle. After all, I had received one twenty years earlier, so why couldn't Dad? There is a passage in the Old Testament about a man called Hezekiah. He had a growth of some kind and was dying. The prophet Isaiah made a poultice of figs and laid it on the affected area. As a result, God gave him an extra fifteen years of life.

Simon and I were both Bible-believing pastors and were willing to give it a try. We stood beside his bed. Simon had the figs and I had a Bible. We placed the figs on his head, prayed and read out the scriptures. I looked up and saw a nurse in the doorway, looking bemused. I don't know what she must have thought, but I didn't care either.

Dad had been on a drip and a feeding tube for several weeks. One day I was sitting at his bedside and I put my hand on his arm. Except it wasn't his arm, it was his thigh. I realised with a jolt how much weight he had lost. He had wasted away to the point where my hand could stretch around his whole leg. I realised that the size of the miracle we needed was getting bigger every day.

I finally began to accept Dad's impending death. The family was called to his bedside several times over the weeks that followed as the medics expected him to die at any moment, but he always rallied and improved when we were there.

Well before Dad had been taken ill I had booked a weekend away. We had planned to camp at a Christian festival. The date was fast approaching. I didn't really feel like going, but we went every year. Mum encouraged me to

All Things Worked Together for Good

go despite Dad's condition, so we travelled down to the site and set up camp. We knew many people who went every year and it was always good to catch up.

My heart was heavy, and I expected the phone to ring at any moment. I couldn't concentrate in the meetings, so I would go and sit in the car and think about him. On the afternoon of the second day the phone rang. It was John, and he sounded subdued. I waited for the words that I knew he was going to say: "He's gone."

I didn't really know what to do. I told the rest of the group, Janey, the boys and some people from church. They left me alone so I could come to terms with what had happened. I walked across the fields thinking about Dad with tears streaming down my face. He died on August 27, 2005, which also happened to be our wedding anniversary.

Later on, I thought about what I would have done if we had still been living in New Zealand. Would I have come back as soon as Dad was taken ill? How would we have paid the rent? There had been eight weeks of uncertainty and distress before he had finally passed away. How hard would that have been? I was thankful for the four years we had spent with him since returning home.

A year or so later, David and I bought a fishing boat between us. We bought lifejackets and a VHF radio, and made sure the boat was seaworthy. One thing Dad had taught us was to respect the sea. David had also been a Lifeboat volunteer, so he had been well trained. The boat was a fibreglass hulled dory; a good size with a 70hp Evinrude motor on the back. It was great fun.

James Ricketts

I took some of my colleagues out fishing after work one day. There were five of us. There was a good fishing spot a few miles away round the coast, so I pushed the throttle forward and we surged ahead. The boat would do forty knots on a calm day. After an hour or so, no one had caught anything. We all had mackerel feathers: six hooks with coloured feathers attached to a trace with a weight attached.

I looked across to the rocks and saw that people were catching fish there. As I looked down the boat, I noticed that everyone, including myself, had their rods over the starboard side. I ordered everyone to reel their lines in. They looked at me curiously and said, "Whatever you say. You're the skipper!"

Once everyone had their line reeled in, I said: "Right, everyone turn around and cast your lines out on the other side of the boat." I don't know why I did this. I was just having a laugh really. But God, it seems, had an even bigger one.

As soon as we dropped our lines down on the port side, the fish started biting and before long the boat was full. There was no point taking more fish than could be used, so we stopped fishing. Even after throwing the smaller ones back there were about a hundred and fifty mackerel in the boat. One of the guys said to me, "Hey, isn't there something about this in the Bible?"

He was right, of course. There is a story just like this in the Gospels. Some of the disciples were fishermen and had been out all night but caught nothing. Jesus was on the beach as they were coming back in to shore empty-handed.

All Things Worked Together for Good

"Go back out and this time cast your nets out on the other side of the boat," he told them.

They obeyed, albeit reluctantly, and the resultant catch was so great that their nets began to break. Another boat had to come alongside and help land the fish.

I was always applying for promotions at work. After several attempts I was given a staff job, which involved planning the up-and-coming jobs for the various trades in the department. I would then have to prepare a schedule for the weeks ahead so that all the workers had jobs that could be issued to them every day.

At first I quite enjoyed it. It was a nice, clean environment, with no more hot, dusty work. There was a lot to do with meetings to go to, schedules to prepare, work to be planned and contractors to be organised. The list went on. It was like cooking on a range stove with about eight saucepans on the go at once, endlessly trying to juggle the many tasks. Aside from this, I found myself playing 'piggy in the middle'. I was hassled by the tradesmen and also given grief by upper management. It was no picnic.

The job was office-based, so I wasn't as active as I had been on the tools. I would often find myself reaching for snacks: biscuits in the drawer and cakes in the fridge. Before long, I was unfit and overweight. In fact, I was heavier than I had ever been. Something had to be done.

I started eating fruit instead and bought a treadmill, which I set up in the conservatory. I had always wanted to run. The closest I had ever got to it was when I trained with Simon before he joined the police, and that had only been a mile and a half. I would watch enviously as athletic-looking people ran along the paths and lanes near our house.

To start with I could only manage a few minutes on the treadmill, but before long I could run for an hour without stopping. To avoid the boredom, I put a TV in front of the treadmill and would watch it as I plodded along. Sometimes I would venture outside and run around the scenic coastal pathways and roads on the island. It felt so good and freeing to be able to do this.

A few years later my cousin Peter, a keen runner, talked me into entering a half-marathon. At thirteen miles, I must have been mad! However, I felt fantastic after doing the race. What an achievement! I quickly booked another later in the year. I soon found that running was quite addictive. Sometimes on a Sunday afternoon I would run for two or three hours, covering up to twenty miles.

After being in ministry in Holyhead for seven years, I was informed by my overseer that I should take a sabbatical. As I was in full-time employment as well as in ministry, this wasn't straightforward. Usually, a sabbatical would be a three-month break from pastoral duties in order to reflect and contemplate; a way of recharging the batteries, so to speak. My overseer recommended that I took a few weeks off at least.

I knew exactly where I needed to go. New Zealand was calling me. Janey had gone on a trip to Israel that year with some friends and attended a conference in Canada, so she fully supported the idea of me going away for three weeks by myself. I spoke with my friend Mark in Auckland and we agreed on a suitable date. Then I booked my flights. It had been eight years since I had been in New Zealand, and I was excited about returning. I made preparations to travel that autumn.

The day finally arrived for me to embark on my trip. I had made a few plans and arranged a cheap rental car. Mark had agreed to accommodate me so I could use his home as a base and travel around as I wanted. A friend whom I had not seen since my youth group days, when we had attended meetings with the youth group in Liverpool, had since moved to Christchurch. I decided to book an internal flight from Auckland to stay with him for a weekend.

David drove me to Manchester to catch my shuttle to Heathrow. It felt strange making my way to New Zealand again, particularly as I was travelling alone. Long-haul flights like this were no big deal for me by this point. I settled in for the long flight to Singapore and even managed to sleep for a few hours. My final flight touched down in Auckland close to midnight, and Mark picked me up and drove me to his house. I was finally there.

I bought a small notebook and pen so I could write down everything God said to me. Mark was busy working, so I picked up my rental car and ended up walking on Milford beach, near the apartment we had once lived in. It struck me as I walked along the beach that we all strive so much. The Bible teaches that we are like sons and daughters to God, but we behave as if we are servants. We rush around trying our best not to upset Him.

The prodigal son returned to the father, willing to become his servant. Bu the father recognised him as a son and he was treated as such. This is a simple truth; a basic part of Christian doctrine. For some reason, I had missed it or thought it didn't apply to me. God spoke to me very clearly as I walked on the beach that day and I wrote lots of notes in my journal.

A few days later, Mark told me about a group he attended every week, which was held at the home of a pastor and his wife. His wife was a qualified counsellor and had done lots of research and written books on the subject of counselling. I agreed to go along and see what it was all about.

I sat in the corner while the other people in the room were being trained in a particular method of counselling that involved asking leading questions. As I was a visitor, I was asked if I minded being a kind of guinea pig. I agreed. After all, it was only a training session.

The questions were designed to make the person think about where God was in his or her life. The answer to each question would lead to another question. I resisted the temptation to give textbook answers and tried to be as honest as I could. All I remember is that I started weeping. God was clearly doing something in my life. I went along to the group with Mark over the next couple of weeks and really lost some of my baggage.

The day after that first session I picked up a motorcycle from a rental place on the North Shore. I had asked for a medium-sized machine. When I arrived, they told me that a big 1200cc machine had just come back and asked if I would mind taking that instead. Would I ever?! They gave me all the protective gear, and off I went. I decided to just take off for a few days and go wherever the feeling took me. I knew Janey wouldn't be pleased when she found out, but it was something I had to do.

All Things Worked Together for Good

I went back to Mark's house and packed a few things. I had decided to head in a southward direction. The big Suzuki bike was fantastic; the kind of machine I could only dream of owning. I had ridden bikes for a while after my major accident, but there had understandably come a time when Janey didn't want me to ride bikes any more.

Over the years I had visited my old friend Stuart, who had moved away from the Holyhead area, from time to time. He had a big bike and I had been known to take it out for a spin, so I wasn't completely out of practice.

So I set off down the Southern Motorway and on to State Highway 1. The speed limit is 100 kmh in New Zealand, which equates to 62 mph. Having been stopped for speeding when I lived there, I wanted to be cautious. I looked down at the speedometer and saw that it indicated 100 mph. I then realised the speedo was in miles per hour, not kilometres per hour, which put me at 60 kmh over the speed limit. Whoops! I returned to a speed that was within the legal limit and continued with a huge smile on my face.

I found myself in the town where my first church had been. I called on the elder, a man I had not always seen eye to eye with. We had lunch together and spoke about our respective lives, but it was all a bit superficial.

I started putting my bike gear back on in readiness to go, but then I felt there was something else I needed to do. I sat down again and apologised to him and his wife for anything I might have done to upset them while I was their pastor. We talked some more and prayed together. Then I headed off, feeling I had got rid of more baggage.

I carried on riding, calling in at Rotorua and then heading on to Taupo with its huge lake. I found a backpackers' lodge in a nice location and decided to stay the night. Mark had given me the number of a couple who had visited my church a few years previously and were living in Taupo. I had called them earlier in the day but they were out, so I had left a voicemail. They returned my call, came to the place where I was staying and took me out for coffee.

The next morning I headed back to Rotorua, as it was a good place to stop for breakfast. The roads in this area were quiet and I was really enjoying the ride. I started thinking about my trip and the things God had said to me. I started to feel a bit guilty about riding the bike when I heard the voice of God.

"Enjoy it, son," he seemed to be saying to me.

I learned a lot about God and sonship during this trip. I stopped for breakfast and then continued back up to Auckland.

A couple of days later I returned the bike to the shop and picked up my rental car. As soon as I had returned the bike I called Janey and told her about my riding experience. She wasn't happy about it, but I was safe and sound and had returned the bike, so there was nothing to worry about.

The next stop was the airport for my flight down to Christchurch. On the way there, I was challenged by God to write down all the negative things I had believed about myself. I stopped the car and began to write. It turned out there was quite a long list. I sensed God saying to me that these were lies. I felt challenged to believe the truth about myself from God's perspective. I began to write another list. By the end of the exercise, more baggage was gone.

I was sitting in the departure lounge of the domestic terminal waiting for my flight to board when I noticed a

All Things Worked Together for Good

familiar face walking in. It was the pastor of one of the New Zealand churches, whom I had encountered a few times. I couldn't say I liked him; in fact, we didn't really get on.

I called out his name and he turned to face me with a surprised look on his face. He shook my hand and we chatted for a while. It transpired that he was no longer a pastor, but some kind of financial advisor. I was finally able to get rid of a lot of negative thoughts and opinions I had held about this man. Even more baggage offloaded!

My journal was filling up and the day of my departure was drawing closer. Before taking the trip, I had really had no idea how the trip would work out as a sabbatical. Nothing had really been planned, but I believe God set all these situations up for me as I went from place to place. I had driven around some of the places that had held some significance for us. I felt guilty that we had moved so much and the boys' education had been disrupted.

My last day arrived, and Mark drove me to the airport and saw me off. I had a relaxing flight back, managing a few hours' sleep once again. I had a few hours between flights at Singapore and a colleague had given me a tip. There was a hotel within the airport complex, and for a few dollars it was possible to have a jacuzzi and a swim in the roof pool. It was midnight and the temperature was still thirty degrees.

David kindly picked me up from the airport and drove me back. It's always nice to be back home. Of course, Janey and the boys wanted to know all about the trip, and I got a little telling off about the motorcycle adventure.

It was Saturday night, which meant it was time for sermon preparation to begin. However, God had spoken to me so much while I was in New Zealand that I had plenty to say.

A few years previously, Janey had bought me a surprise Christmas present. I had torn the wrapping paper off and looked at the hinged black case. 'Surely not?' I had thought, but yes it was! A trumpet! It had been about twenty-five years since I had handed back the instrument I had learned to play at school. I had eagerly taken it out of the case and blown a few scales, then played a couple of tunes I still knew off by heart. Sadly, it had then gone back into its case and stayed there for a long time.

News arrived that the aluminium smelter where I had first learned my trade and spent a further eight years was closing down. It had been deemed unprofitable and hundreds of jobs were on the line. The date was set, and support was given to the soon-to-be redundant workers. Employment consultants and recruitment advisors were drafted in to help workers prepare their CVs and apply for jobs. This was to be a major crossroads in my life.

The church had been in decline for the past couple of years. After eight years in ministry there, I doubted it could be turned around under my leadership. I decided that I would step down from the church leadership at the same time my job at the aluminium smelter finished. It would be a clean break, a fresh start. Who knew what might be in store for me? I gave notice to the church and began applying for jobs.

After stepping down from church leadership, we decided it would not be fair to the church or the new leader for us to remain there, so we started attending another church in

All Things Worked Together for Good

Bangor. No one knew us, so we had some degree of anonymity there.

One day, I got quite a surprise. Sometimes in church someone might receive 'a word' from God. Sometimes it's a prophesy, other times it's a word of encouragement or a word of knowledge.

One of the people at the front said into the microphone: "I see a shiny trumpet in a case."

That got my attention, and my ears pricked up.

"It's very shiny because it never gets played," the speaker continued.

I know this could be interpreted to mean that someone had spiritual gifts or abilities that were lying dormant, but I also knew exactly what it meant for me. Nobody there really knew us, so this seemed to be a direct word from God for me.

My thoughts returned to the trumpet Janey had bought me, which was still in its case, shiny and new, having never really been played. As soon as I got home I took it out of its case, oiled the valves and began playing. Music books were bought, and I started learning to sight-read written music again. I was a bit rusty, but it was still there somewhere.

After a few weeks of playing it, I began to think I would benefit from having someone to teach me. There was only so much I could do on my own. I made some enquiries, but there was no one nearby who was able to help. A few weeks later I spotted a familiar face at the supermarket. Tim had been the store man at the aluminium smelter. He also happened to be my next-door neighbour.

"Is someone in your house learning to play the trumpet?" he asked.

"Yes," I replied sheepishly, knowing that it must have sounded bad over the garden wall. "It's me."

I had thought I knew Tim quite well. I had often had to go to the main stores and we had frequently shared a laugh and a joke over the counter. We also had neighbourly chats over the garden wall.

So I was taken by surprise when he told me he was a member of the Menai Bridge Brass Band. He was a trombone player but had also played valve instruments, such as the trumpet and cornet. I didn't even have to ask the question; he offered to come round and give me some tuition. I had been looking for someone to teach me and had even considered contacting Bangor University, and here was someone right on my doorstep, literally.

Tim came round the following week with a bundle of music under his arm. Week after week he would come. We would work on various pieces, sometimes ones he brought and sometimes tunes I wanted to play. I began trying to play jazz, albeit not very well and with a hopeless sense of timing. I eventually became a regular player at a jazz club, but I struggled. The first time I was asked to play a solo, I stood up to play but was so nervous I couldn't even produce a note. I stood there silently, feeling humiliated.

Tim tried to help me with my timing issues, but I just couldn't seem to grasp it. However, if I played the same piece on my bass I could play it with my eyes closed and in perfect time. The problem with playing an instrument like the trumpet is that so much effort is used to produce the sound that there isn't much brain power left to think about timing! That was my excuse, anyway.

All Things Worked Together for Good

I figured that if I joined the brass band Tim was a part of, I would learn to keep time and also improve my music reading skills. Playing in a brass band involves strict discipline. Unlike jazz, timing and sight-reading are critical skills. To start with, I thought of it as a means to an end; the end being to improve my jazz playing.

The band held concerts and played in various competitions around the country. This was a serious group of musicians. Rehearsals were held twice a week and they would play hymns to warm up. I liked this, as I knew most of the tunes from years of being in church. Slowly and surely, my timing and sight-reading improved.

I became a regular, paid-up member and even took part in competitions and concerts. One year we even reached the national finals. Our band had won the semi-finals and was representing Wales. That made me feel proud and gave me a huge sense of achievement. Despite my intention of joining the band just to improve my timing and discipline, I had to admit that I was enjoying the band experience.

Handing back my instrument as I left school, I never dreamed that thirty-odd years later I would be playing it again. I don't know where it will lead. Sometimes I play in church and I have even joined a jazz band. All this came about because of a word spoken in obedience to God's prompting during a church service. God never fails to surprise me.

James Ricketts

Postscript

I am still working as an electrician in my home town today. I'm an active member of my home church and as busy as ever with my musical commitments. I still enjoy running but haven't raced for a while. We have just moved house again, hopefully for the last time. Generally, life is good.

Janey recently took up painting. She had always regretted not going to Art College, so it's good to see her artistic flair coming into its own. She has sold some of her paintings and has prints for sale locally and sometimes takes part in exhibitions.

Phil moved away to the Midlands to pursue a career in graphic design and now runs a successful business.

Paul has developed a passion for gardening. He looks after an allotment and the garden at our new home. He has a wealth of knowledge on the subject and is well known by other gardeners. He won a best allotment prize one year.

I often think of the verse I have used in the title of this book. Despite all the difficulties, the conflicts, the pain and the hurts, the bigger picture is greater. Our challenges shape and prepare us for the next chapter in life. Present-day struggles will pass and become history. They will play their part in forming us, and in developing character and strength.

It's easy to lose heart and become discouraged when things get tough, but try to think of it like a jigsaw puzzle. The pieces are all made up of strange shapes and sometimes we have no clear idea of where they fit. However, jigsaw pieces are only a small part of the bigger picture. As our lives continue, the bigger picture starts to emerge.

I often look at my keyring, which now holds both halves of the fifty pence piece. It's good to look back, but it's even better to look forward.

If you have any questions about anything you have read or want more information, please feel free to contact me at revjamesricketts@gmail.com and I will endeavour to respond.

Printed in Great Britain
by Amazon